Oxford Primary Social Studies

Knowing My Region

5

Pat Lunt

OXFORD
UNIVERSITY PRESS

Contents

1 Culture and identity

In this unit you will learn:

- why families are important
- to understand your own identity
- how to write a self-assessment and a report
- to make accurate drawings and plans
- about the cultures of our region and their many different features.

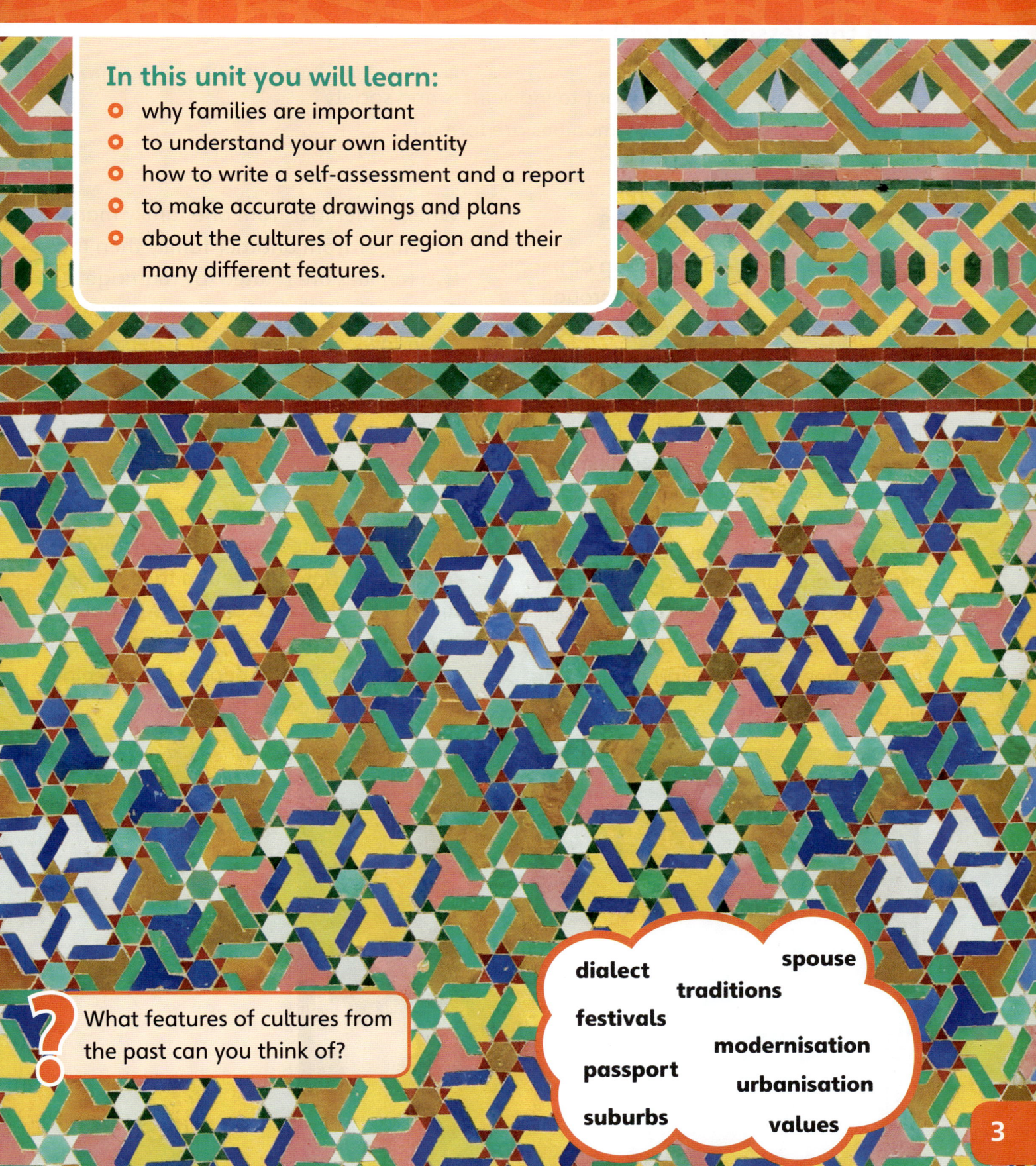

What features of cultures from the past can you think of?

dialect
spouse
traditions
festivals
modernisation
passport
urbanisation
suburbs
values

1.1 The importance of family

In this lesson you will learn:
- to create a family tree
- why families are important to individuals and society
- to understand how communities are formed.

Family relationships

A family is formed from a group of people who are related 'by blood' or through marriage. People in this group are known as 'kin' and the relationships they have are called 'kinship'.

Blood relationships are those between people who can trace a direct line of ancestors or descendants. A young person is related 'by blood' to his or her parents and siblings, aunts and uncles, grandparents and great-grandparents. The blood relatives of an older person would include his or her children, nieces and nephews, grandchildren and great-grandchildren.

When a member from one family marries a member from another family then those two families are related 'by marriage'. The people in these families are known as 'in-laws'. The parents of a person's **spouse** are parents-in-law. If a person's spouse has brothers and sisters these will be brothers-in-law and sisters-in-law.

In most societies there are special rules about the relationships that people who are closely related can have. In Islam, a woman is only allowed to take off her hijab in the presence of certain people, known as her *maharim*. There are special rules, too, about the people a particular individual is allowed to marry.

◀ When people marry they become members of one another's family and are related by marriage.

A family tree

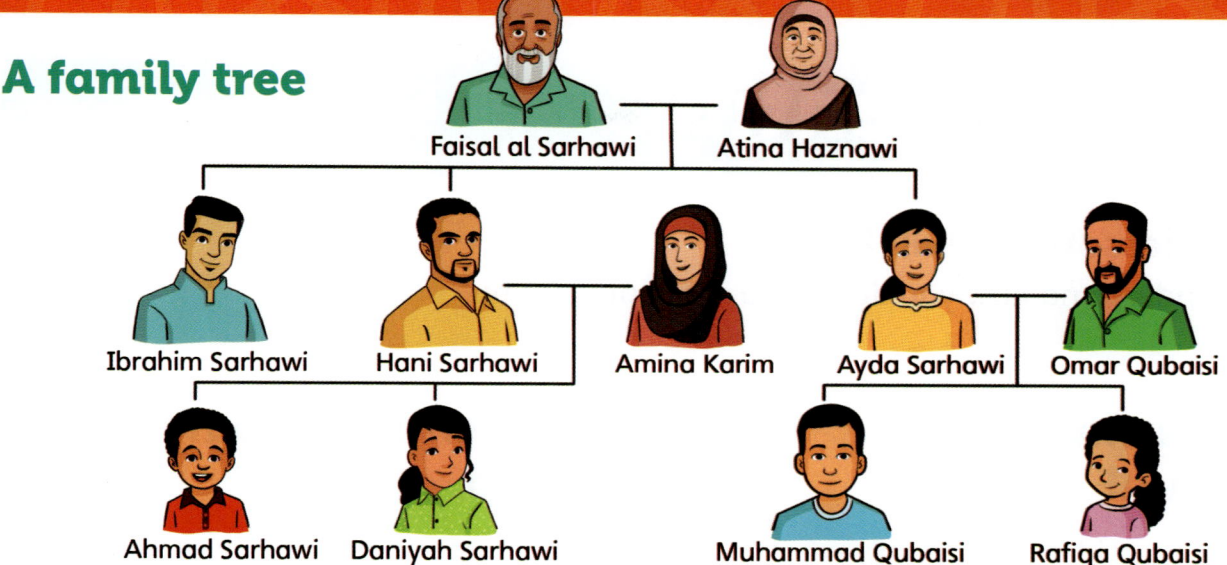

Faisal al Sarhawi — Atina Haznawi

Ibrahim Sarhawi   Hani Sarhawi   Amina Karim   Ayda Sarhawi   Omar Qubaisi

Ahmad Sarhawi   Daniyah Sarhawi   Muhammad Qubaisi   Rafiqa Qubaisi

▲ A family tree is a special diagram that shows how individual members of a family are related.

The family in society

The family has many important roles in society. It is a social unit in which people experience love and acceptance. The family gives its members a feeling of belonging and it helps them to create their sense of identity.

The family also offers help and guidance as children develop their own personalities, characteristics and attitudes. It is also generally understood that parents are responsible for the socialisation of their children. This means that parents should teach their children about the society they live in and about the kind of behaviour that the society expects. Part of socialisation is learning about the culture and customs of a society and about the values that are understood to be important.

Individuals in a family learn to relate to people of different ages. As families live and mix together, the range of people in a person's experience grows and so they develop skills and attitudes that will help them in the wider society.

▲ Children learn many things from their parents and older relations, including expectations about behaviour.

Activities

1 Describe relationships shown in the family tree that involve grandparents and grandchildren, nieces and nephews, uncles and aunts and in-laws.

2 Work in a group to discuss things you have learnt from your family.

1.2 Your identity

In this lesson you will learn:
- to understand how you develop a sense of identity.

Your identity as an individual

In a sense, your identity is simply *who you are*. Some official documents, such as a **passport**, are a 'proof' of your identity. This means the document proves that you are the particular person who you say you are. Such a document will state your given names and your family name, and this is 'who you are'.

In another sense, your identity is not simply about who you *say* you are but the person that you *think* you are. This part of your identity is based on your qualities and characteristics and the way you relate to other people. You might see yourself as someone who is kind or quiet, lively or adventurous. You may also think that you are confident, shy or friendly when relating to other people.

▲ It may not be so easy to answer the question, 'Who do you think you are?'

Your identity as part of a group

Part of your personal identity comes from belonging to a family. This is why you have a surname or family name. People also often share a group identity or common identity with other people, and this becomes part of who they are too.

Identifying with other people can be based on the fact that people are from the same ethnic groups. This is the group of people who share a common national or cultural heritage. People from the same nation often share similar ideas about how society should operate and how people should behave.

People with a common culture often share things, such as styles of dress and cooking, language, beliefs and behaviour. A member of that group therefore identifies him or herself as being part of that culture.

▲ The Maasai people of East Africa identify strongly with their cultural group.

Developing your identity

Your identity as a member of a family or as a person from a particular country is fixed. Your attitudes, qualities and characteristics are not. These parts of your personal identity continue to develop as you grow older but they are influenced by many things, including your family, your friendship groups and your culture.

Parents pass on traditions, customs, values and other aspects of culture to their children, which they hope will help them to be good members of society.

Children also need to learn to think for themselves, especially as they experience other influences from outside the family, for example through peer groups, television or the internet. It is important to be aware of the influences around you and to know how you will react to them, because not all of them are helpful.

Did you know?

Some surveys suggest that many people in modern societies watch between 25 and 35 hours of television each week, which is longer than some people work.

▲ What influences do you think there are on people as they think about their identity?

Activities

1 Make a personal profile which explains who you think you are in terms of your cultural and national identity.

2 Identify and discuss the groups you belong to and how each one influences you.

1.3 Thinking skills

In this lesson you will learn:
- ○ to identify different thinking skills
- ○ to identify and assess personal capabilities

As your identity develops, you begin to form your own opinions. You can think about what is right or wrong, whether something is fair or not, and which things in life are truly important to you. You also develop personal skills and capabilities that will help you learn and interact with others.

Managing yourself

Everyone thinks, feels and reacts in particular ways at different times. Understanding how we react and behave in different situations helps us to decide if these reactions or behaviours are helpful or not. Understanding these aspects of our personality helps us to make the most of any situation.

Knowing your strengths lets you make the most of them. Identifying areas that need improvement helps you to set goals for improvement and to focus on achieving them.

Managing yourself is also about understanding how you organise your time and plan out the things that need to be done. It is important to remember that everyone organises and plans in different ways and you should find the right way for you.

▲ Some people love the idea of taking on a new challenge.

Dealing with information

Learning to deal with information is an important skill because we receive so much information every day. We should know how to find out the information we need, how to decide what information is useful, how best to record the information, and how to make use of it.

▲ There is a huge amount of information available today. We have to learn how to pick out what we need.

Thinking

Thinking is obviously a part of dealing with information. Thinking helps decide what information you need and how to get it. Critical thinking helps you to evaluate the information you have: is it true, is it a fact, or is it simply someone's opinion? Thinking also helps you to decide how any new information fits with information you already have, and what you might be able to do with the new information. It also helps when you have to make decisions.

Creative thinking helps you to make connections between different pieces of information, and to come up with solutions to problems.

Activity

Write a self-assessment that describes some of your strengths and areas for development. Think about:

- subjects in school where you feel more and less confident

- how well you cope when facing new challenges

- situations when you react well and situations when your reactions are not so helpful

- whether you are able to persevere with something difficult

- whether you use effective methods to find information

- how well-organised you think you are

- whether you can think creatively and come up with new ideas or solutions to problems.

1.4 Our cultural heritage 1

In these lessons you will learn:

- why we study the past
- about the development of the culture of the countries of the Arabian Gulf.

Why study the past?

A culture is the way of life of a people, shown in the activities, beliefs and practices of the population. These are often based on very long-standing traditions and values from the past. Our lives are greatly influenced by the culture in which we live, so it is good to understand how it is formed.

We study the past to help us understand why we live the way we do in the present. When we study the cultures of the past we can see how they have helped to create the culture we live in today. We are able to find parts of our past that should be valued and celebrated. Understanding our cultural heritage also helps us to decide which modern influences on our culture are positive and which are not.

History

History is the study of the past and it tells us about things that have happened in the past.

The primary sources for understanding history are the objects, documents and creative works that people have left behind. The objects might be simple things such as arrowheads or pieces of pottery.

They can be the ruins of a single building or the remains of a great city. The documents might be lists of treasures received by a great king or the accounts of a grain trader in an ancient port. Creative works are works of art, many of which reveal important information about life at the time when they were created.

▲ What does this piece of pottery from Ancient Greece tell us about life in those times?

Historians use all this evidence to provide clues that help them put together a picture of what life was like in the past.

Why are there different cultures?

We all belong to one race which is called the human race. In the distant past people moved to live in different parts of the world. Differences between these people and the way they lived came about because of the conditions created by the **climate** in the various different places to which they moved. These affected the kind of food that was available, the sorts of houses the people needed to build, and the clothes they needed to wear.

As the different groups lived together they created their own languages and exchanged ideas. They developed different ways of living, with some people working as farmers, fishermen and craftspeople and others becoming traders, government officials and leaders. Others created works of art, told stories, sang songs and invented dances that reflected their experiences.

▲ How would life have developed for people who lived in this kind of environment?

Cultural history

Cultural history is concerned particularly with how a culture was expressed in the past. The expressions of a culture include language, beliefs, songs, dances, food, clothing, houses, community groups and traditions. Many of these parts of cultural expression are handed down from one generation to another and in this way they last for many hundreds or even thousands of years.

▲ What aspects of a past culture can special buildings reveal?

How civilisations develop

A civilisation has certain characteristics, including special achievements, advances in knowledge, learning and artistic expression set within a system of shared beliefs and customs. How does a civilisation develop?

Early groups of people grew in number, which made them stronger. They would first use this strength to control the environment to provide the things they needed for survival. If the group needed more resources it could trade with another group or overpower the other group and claim its land.

Groups of people eventually joined together to form communities. Sometimes one group within the community would be stronger than the others and they would create a kingdom. If a ruler became powerful enough then he could spread the influence of his country over many others and create an empire.

In a long-lasting empire people begin to use the same language and develop ways of living that are similar. Practical

things like clothing and the use of standard weights, measures and money also spread. Ideas are shared across large areas and works of art are created in a similar style.

The Aztecs in South America, the Ancient Egyptians, Ancient Greeks and Ancient Romans are examples of past civilisations.

The cultural heritage of the Arabian Gulf

The cultures of the Arabian Peninsula have a heritage based largely on two things: the traditions of the Arab people and the faith of Islam. The Arab people have strong traditions of hospitality, generosity and family solidarity. The arrival of Islam brought different tribes together and established a unity among them as they followed a common religion.

Activities

1 Work in a group to discuss the differences you would expect to see in the food, clothing and shelter of the early cultures that developed in the different climate zones. Explain the reasons for these differences.

2 Work in a group to find out about a civilisation from history. Find out where the civilisation was founded, how long it lasted, and identify two of its major achievements.

1.6 Language and calligraphy

In this lesson you will learn:

○ about the importance of language and calligraphy in Arabic culture.

Language

As ancient people moved and settled in different parts of the world they developed separate languages. The languages of the people who settled in the Arabian Peninsula finally developed into Arabic. An early form of the language, now called Classical Arabic, was originally developed for the creation of poetry. It was only spoken and not written.

Eventually a written form was developed and used for the texts of the Qur'an, for works of literature and for texts on mathematics, science, medicine and astronomy.

▲ Books were created using the common written form of Arabic. These could be read by anyone in the Muslim Empire.

Arabic spread with the Muslim conquests of the 7th century and became the official language of the Muslim empire. The influence of the languages that already existed in different parts of the empire meant that spoken Arabic developed in slightly different ways in the various parts of the Muslim world. Particular forms of a language are called **dialects**, and the dialects of Arabic are known as 'colloquial Arabic'.

The variation in the spoken language could have caused some problems for traders and others. The written form was the same everywhere, however, which meant that people could communicate across the whole empire. More importantly, it stood as a symbol of the unity of all Muslims.

The written form of Arabic used today, which is known as Modern Standard Arabic, is a continuation of Classical Arabic, with some changes to grammar and the addition of modern vocabulary.

Whatever form it takes, the Arabic language is always held in high esteem and is greatly valued as the medium of a rich cultural heritage.

▲ Arabic is used all the time in the everyday life of Arab nations and peoples.

Calligraphy

Calligraphy is a decorative art form based on writing. Just as different languages developed in various parts of the world, so there are different forms of calligraphy. In many cases these are seen to be important aspects of culture. This is certainly true of Islamic calligraphy which developed alongside the writing of the Qur'an and the Arabic language. Part of its importance is that it uses the form of the language that is shared by all Muslims. For many people it has a special spiritual significance.

Islamic calligraphy is found on many ancient objects such as coins and tiles, and as an element within other art forms.

▲ Calligraphy is still used decoratively in architecture.

Activities

1 Work in a group to discuss why it would be of benefit for people to be able to communicate with one another, in writing and speech, throughout the whole Muslim Empire.

2 Make a careful copy of a piece of Islamic calligraphy.

1.7 Islamic art

In this lesson you will learn:
○ about the importance of art in cultures of the Arabian Gulf.

Islamic art

Traditional Islamic art is an important feature of the cultural heritage of the Arabian Gulf countries and still influences artists today. Art within Islam developed a very distinctive style that used designs and patterns rather than images that were meant to look like real-life objects and creatures. This happened because in the early days of Islam the believers were in conflict with people who worshipped idols. There was a fear that if art included pictures of people and animals then people might worship these images instead of Allah.

Islamic art is often brightly coloured and based on images of flowers and plants. These images are used in repeating patterns to create very elaborate designs. These designs always seek to express ideas, beliefs and values from Islamic cultures. However, Islamic art is not limited to what can be called 'religious art'. It is found on objects used in all parts of life, such as household objects including vases, jugs, lanterns and glasses. It is also found on decorative items such as wall tiles, rugs and carpets. Every time one of these objects is used it reminds the believer that Islam is a part of every aspect of life.

◀ Objects to be used every day were often decorated with intricate designs.

Ceramics

Ceramics are articles made from clay that have been hardened by heating at high temperatures. Ceramics include 'pottery' items such as vases, plates and dishes and also tiles.

▲ Ceramic tiles were used to create beautiful, intricate designs.

Glassware

The production of glassware was an important feature of the Muslim empire for almost 500 years from the 800s onwards. Glass was used to create many objects including beakers, jars, bowls, jugs and mosque lamps.

▲ Mosque lamps were often inscribed with verses from the Qur'an.

Rugs and carpets

Carpet weaving is an important part of Islamic cultures and possibly goes back to the pre-Islamic traditions of the nomadic Arabs who used rugs as furniture because they were easy to pack away. They have been used as floor coverings and wall hangings and also as religious objects, in the form of prayer mats.

Metalwork

Highly-skilled metalworkers created heavily decorated objects such as candlesticks, lampstands, bowls, dishes and caskets and also became involved in the creation of scientific instruments.

Activities

1   Work in a group to discuss what is distinctive about Islamic art.

2   Write a short report about the place of art in Islamic culture.

1.8 Islamic architecture

In this lesson you will learn:
○ about the importance of architecture in cultures of the Arabian Gulf.

Architecture

Buildings and other structures are described as architecture. They are created to have particular functions but they should also be pleasing to look at and express ideas that are important to the society in which they appear. For this reason they are important symbols of a culture and in some cases are works of art. The buildings that are perhaps the most characteristic example of Islamic architecture are mosques.

Mosques have been an important part of Muslim settlements since the beginning of Islam. The first mosque was built by prophet Muhammad (Peace Be Upon Him) in Madinah. He built several small huts for himself and his followers around a central courtyard. The courtyard was a place of prayer and meeting. Here, visitors could rest and the poor received food and refreshment. This simple pattern has been the basis of mosque design ever since.

A mosque functions as a place of meeting, prayer and study. There are rooms for these activities, and other facilities that allow for such things as the ritual washing before prayer. Another practical requirement is the need to call believers to prayer. This is done from a minaret which is a tall tower, raised above ground level to allow the call to be heard from a distance.

◀ The call to prayer is delivered from a minaret.

Did you know?

The Selimiye Mosque in Turkey was finished in 1575 and has a dome with a diameter of over 31 metres.

A mosque should look beautiful and turn the believers' thoughts to Allah. Mosques are often covered in designs typical of Islamic art which feature repeating geometric patterns. These are intended to suggest the infinity that is beyond the material world. The other major symbolic feature of the mosque is the dome which, internally, represents the universe.

Other important buildings in Islamic architecture are forts, tombs and palaces. The style of architecture used in these great buildings was taken and adapted for use in other public buildings and in houses.

Landscape architecture

Landscape architecture is about the design of outdoor spaces and gardens, which have always been important to Muslims. This importance is reflected in famous Islamic gardens in places such as the Taj Mahal in India and the Alhambra in Spain, and in the desire for beautiful public parks and gardens in today's modern cities.

▲ Gardens have always been important in Islamic societies, as here at the Taj Mahal in India.

▲ The Museum of Islamic Art, Doha.

Activities

1 Design a building or a garden that has Islamic elements.

2 Find out about three buildings or structures in your country and explain why they are good examples of Islamic architecture.

In this lesson you will learn:
○ about the importance of music, drama and dance in cultures of the Arabian Gulf.

Music

Early pre-Islamic music in the Arabian Peninsula was associated with the poets who developed language to create poetry. These poems were recited by the poets themselves and were also sung by others.

The arrival and acceptance of Islam over a wide area created some stability within society. This allowed for developments in many areas of culture, including music. The way in which music was thought about and written down became more complex. New instruments were created and others were adapted. Musical ideas travelled to all the areas covered by the spread of Islam.

Early instruments included the *oud*, the *rebab*, the *qanon*, the *nay* and several types of drum. These are still important parts of Arabic music.

The recent increase of interest in 'world music' has seen musicians playing traditional Arabic music in concert halls and other venues around the globe.

Arab music has influenced musicians around the world and in recent times has been influenced itself. Many young musicians today are exploring traditional Arabic songs and music and interpreting these in new styles, using both traditional and modern instruments.

Dance

Traditional dances have been an important part of Arab culture for hundreds of years. The dances have long been a feature of **festivals**, holidays, weddings and general gatherings. The dances take a number of forms such as line dances or circle dances and can be performed by men or women only and sometimes by men and women taking part alternately.

Dances such as the *arda* were performed by men at meetings which occurred for different social reasons, including weddings. The *arda* is a war dance which expresses a sense of belonging and loyalty within the tribe. The dancers will also keep up a steady chant and the pace of the dance is maintained by rhythms beaten out on drums and by hand-clapping.

▲ Traditional dances were used to mark special occasions or to remember special events.

A popular dance, performed by women in the United Arab Emirates, is the *na'ashat*. In this dance, a group of women dress in long, colourful robes, tossing their heads rhythmically to make their long hair move from side to side.

There are many dances with many origins and variations in different parts of the region.

Drama

In the times before there were books and when most people were not able to read, there was a strong tradition of storytelling. Professional storytellers would retell popular stories that became important parts of a local culture.

Activity

Work in a group to make a presentation explaining how and why either music or dance is an important part of traditional Arab culture.

1.10 Culture

In this lesson you will learn:
- to think how traditional and modern cultures of the Arabian Gulf countries exist together.

Changes in the built environment

Before the discovery of oil, the countries of the Arabian Gulf had not developed modern economies and most people lived in small towns and villages. Since the 1960s there has been very rapid development and modernisation.

▲ Settlements were quite small and simple before modern development.

Modernisation has also resulted in **urbanisation**, where most of the population live in cities. The architectural features of many of these cities are based on other cities of global importance around the world. Modern cities have skyscrapers in the central business area alongside multi-storey residential buildings full of apartments. There are large shopping malls, public spaces such as squares, parks and gardens, widely spread **suburbs**, a network of highways and other modern transportation links.

▲ The cities of the Arabian Gulf countries are among the newest and fastest-growing in the world. This is Dubai in the UAE.

Modernisation has taken place to provide for the needs of large companies that have been encouraged to establish their business in the area and to help in the continuing development of these countries.

The governments of the Arabian Gulf countries want to see their countries develop and succeed. They also want to make sure that the culture and traditions of Arab Islamic societies are preserved.

For these reasons, modern architects are encouraged to include traditional elements from Islamic architecture in the design of new buildings. There are also initiatives to preserve many old buildings from the past, such as forts, palaces and souks.

City planners know that gardens have always been important in Arabic Islamic cultures and the designs of the new cities include features such as parks, flowerbeds, gardens and even palm groves.

▲ The central market in Abu Dhabi is a very modern design which includes clear references to traditional Islamic art.

Modern cultural influences

Modernisation has brought many advantages. The opportunities for people to study and to work in different occupations have increased dramatically. A wide range of goods is now available for people to buy in modern shopping areas. At the same time, developments in modern communications and global travel have meant that as countries of the Arabian Peninsula open up to the rest of the world, so they are exposed to many influences from different cultures in terms of dress, food, music and lifestyle. It is important that the traditional Arab and Islamic values which are the basis of the cultures of these countries are preserved.

Activity

Work in a group to discuss the influences of modern culture and traditional cultures in today's society. Consider whether these benefit society or not.

Unit 1 Review questions

1   In many countries of the world, families tell stories to remember their past. This is part of the family's:
   a   oral history
   b   social responsibility
   c   household rules
   d   financial security

2   Which of these terms includes all the others?
   a   Language
   b   Music
   c   Culture
   d   Food

3   Your aunt's children are your:
   a   uncles
   b   cousins
   c   nephews
   d   neighbours

4   The parents of a person's spouse are his or her:
   a   step-parents
   b   grandparents
   c   parents-in-law
   d   aunt and uncle

5   A historian might learn something about an ancient people's religious beliefs from the ruins of a:
   a   fort
   b   palace
   c   warehouse
   d   temple

6   Calligraphy is an art form based on:
   a   birds
   b   writing
   c   flowers
   d   sound

7   Draw a family tree diagram that shows three generations of a family and some in-law relations.

8   Name three groups to which you belong. Briefly describe how each group has influenced you.

9   Describe the type of decoration that might be seen in a mosque. Explain why this style of decoration is chosen.

10 Give a brief description of some traditional Arab dances and give two examples of when and where they may be performed.

11 Give two reasons people might give for the importance of performing traditional music, songs and dances.

12 Give three sources of influence in modern culture and say how these influences might affect modern societies.

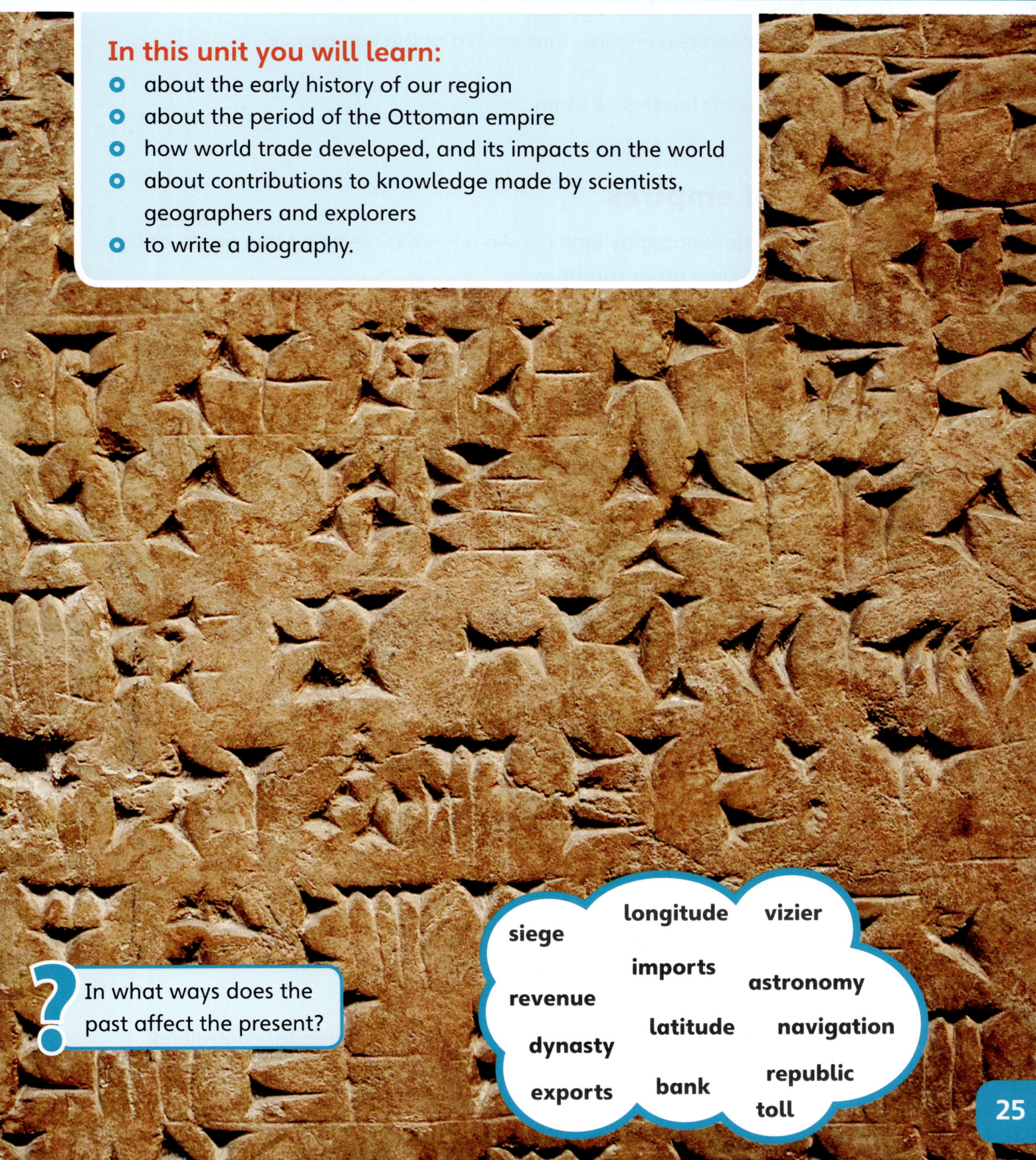

2 History and heritage

In this unit you will learn:
- about the early history of our region
- about the period of the Ottoman empire
- how world trade developed, and its impacts on the world
- about contributions to knowledge made by scientists, geographers and explorers
- to write a biography.

? In what ways does the past affect the present?

siege   longitude   vizier

imports

revenue   astronomy

latitude   navigation

dynasty

exports   bank   republic

toll

2.1 World empires

In this lesson you will learn:

- about the powerful empires that existed at the emergence of Islam
- about the early leaders of Islam.

A history of empires

Human history is dominated by empires. An empire is created when one country extends its control over other countries.

One of the most powerful empires in history was the Roman Empire. This was founded in the ancient city of Rome in Italy in 27BCE. By 117CE it controlled most of western Europe and many lands around the Mediterranean Sea.

In 330CE the Roman emperor Constantine moved the centre of power from Rome to a city called Byzantium. This city was renamed Constantinople and in 395CE the Roman Empire was divided into East and West. The western part of the Empire was invaded by several tribes and eventually collapsed in 495CE. The eastern part became known as the Byzantine Empire.

▲ The Roman Empire in 117CE.

In 527CE, the emperor Justinian came to power. By the time of his death in 565CE, he had added many territories to the Byzantine Empire. A rival empire at the time was the Sassanid Empire which lay to the east.

Both of these empires understood the importance of this area for controlling world trade. The two empires were still in conflict at the emergence of Islam.

The early spread of Islam

Islam spread from its beginnings in Makkah in 610CE. It was largely accepted throughout the Arabian Peninsula by 632CE when prophet Muhammad (Peace Be Upon Him) died. After this, Abu Bakr was appointed as caliph. He was the first of the Rashidite or 'Rightly Guided' caliphs.

Islam expanded under Abu Bakr and under his successor, Umar ibn al-Kattab. Muslims fought against the Byzantine Empire and after the Battle of Yarmouk in 636CE they moved into the lands of modern Syria, Palestine and Lebanon. They also fought the Sassanid Empire and won great victories at the Battle of Qadasiya in 637CE and at the Battle of Nahawand in 642CE.

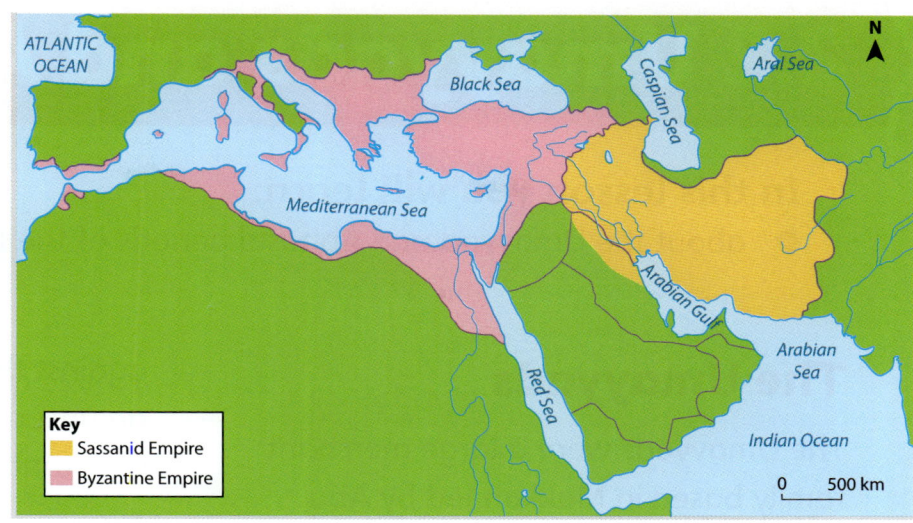

▲ The Byzantine and Sassanid Empires to 600CE.

▲ The expansion of Islam up to 661CE.

Umar died in 644CE and was succeeded by Uthman ibn Affan who ruled for 12 years. In this time the Sassanid Empire was finally won over to Islam and the writings that make up the Qur'an were brought together as a single book.

Ali ibn Abi Talib ruled as the last of the Rashidite caliphs from 656 to 661CE. By this time, Islam had spread into Egypt and along the north coast of Africa.

Activity

Make a timeline showing major events from the founding of the Roman Empire to the end of the rule of the Rashidite caliphs.

2.2 Umayyads and Abbasids

In this lesson you will learn:
- about the Umayyad and Abbasid periods of the Islamic empire.

The Umayyads

The Umayyads were a large merchant family based in Makkah led by Abu Sufyan. Abu Sufyan's son Muawiyah emerged victorious from a civil war that occurred following the death of Uthman ibn Affan and during Ali ibn Abi Talib's reign as caliph. He established himself as the first Ummayad caliph.

The Sufyan's branch of the family ruled from 661 to 684CE and moved the centre of authority to Damascus. Arab unity grew stronger and Islam expanded eastwards into central Asia and north-western India, and west further along the North African coast. There were several campaigns against the Byzantine Empire including an unsuccessful three-year **siege** of Constantinople (674–677CE).

Sufyanid rule came to an end in 684CE and the second branch of the Umayyad family, the Marwanids, took control. Under Abd al-Malik, Islam reached Sind in India and the borders of China in Central Asia. He completed the conquests of North Africa and finally Spain. During this period Arabic became the official state language, communication systems were improved and Arabic coins were introduced. Great achievements in architecture of this period included the building of the Dome of the Rock in Jerusalem (691CE) and the Umayyad Mosque in Damascus (706CE).

▲ The Dome of the Rock in Jerusalem was constructed during the Umayyad period.

▲ Map showing Muslim expansion up to 750CE.

A rival **dynasty**, the Abbasids, overthrew the Umayyad caliphate in 750CE, when the last ruler Marwan II was defeated at the Battle of the Great Zab River. Abu al Abbas al Saffah was proclaimed the first ruler of the Abbasid state.

The Abbasids

The Abbasids moved the capital of the empire from Damascus to Baghdad. The period of Abbasid rule is known for the advancement of knowledge in medicine, mathematics and science and a flourishing of art and literature. All of this was sustained by wealth from continued trade and industry and by tributes paid by subject peoples.

The later period of the Abbasid dynasty also saw the beginnings of a series of campaigns from Europe, known as the Crusades. The Crusaders were able to take the cities of Antioch and Jerusalem which they held for almost a hundred years. In 1187, united under a leader called Salahiddin al-Ayyoubi, the Muslims defeated the Crusaders at the Battle of Hattin and recaptured Jerusalem.

In 1194, Mongol clans under the leadership of a man called Genghis Khan began conquering new territories. The Mongols reached Baghdad in 1258, destroyed the city and killed most of the population, including the last Abbasid caliph.

The Mongols advanced towards Syria to be met there by local armies who were joined by Mamluk forces from Egypt. The Mongols were defeated and expelled from the region in 1260.

Activity

Work in a group to research the Umayyad and Abbasid dynasties. Create a timeline of important events at that time.

2.3 The Ottoman Empire

In this lesson you will learn:
- about the formation of the Ottoman Empire.

The founding of the Ottoman Empire

The Ottoman Empire was founded by Osman I in 1299. His father, Ertugrul, had come to help the Seljuk Turks as they fought on behalf of Islam against the Mongols and the Byzantine Empire. Ertugrul established himself in a village called Sogut in western Anatolia, near the border with the Byzantine Empire.

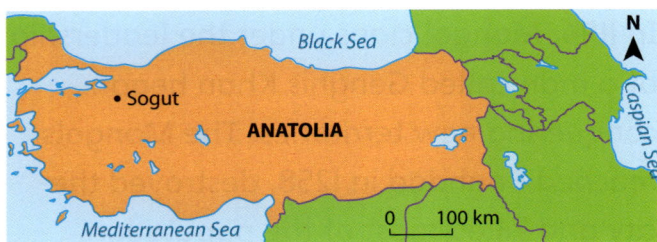

▲ Sogut in Ancient Anatolia saw the beginnings of the Ottoman Empire.

▲ Osman I, the founder of the Ottoman Empire.

The rise of the Ottoman Empire

Osman fought against the Byzantine Empire, taking control of a number of important cities. His son Orhan ruled from 1326 to 1362 and brought the independent states of Anatolia together under one rule. By the end of the 1300s the Ottomans had taken many lands in Europe but had yet to take Constantinople.

In 1402 the Ottomans were attacked in the east by the forces of Timur, a Turkish-Mongolian leader. There was a period of unrest and civil war which ended in 1413 when Mehmet I came to power. Over time, lands that had been lost were re-taken and in 1451 a new sultan, Mehmed II, came to power.

On 6 April 1453, Mehmed II laid siege to Constantinople, surrounding the city and cutting off supplies from land or sea. Over many weeks the Ottoman forces attempted to gain access to the city through tunnels dug beneath the walls, and they made several attacks against the walls. The city was finally overrun on 29 May.

The fall of Constantinople signalled the end of the Byzantine Empire. The city was renamed Istanbul, 'The city of Islam', and became the capital of the Ottoman Empire. Mehmed set about rebuilding the city and people came to live there from all over the Islamic world.

Expansion of the Empire

The Ottomans continued to increase their territories over the next 150 years, turning their attention largely to the Arab world. Under Sultan Selim I they took control of Algeria in North Africa and expanded their frontiers eastwards into Persia and southwards into Egypt and the eastern side of the Arabian Peninsula. Selim was recognised as the protector of the holy cities of Makkah and Madinah.

Selim's successor was Sultan Suleiman the Magnificent. He led conquests of many lands in central Europe, the region of Mesopotamia, and the lands between Egypt and Algeria in North Africa. He took control of sea routes of the Mediterranean, the Red Sea and the Arabian Gulf, and spent large sums of money restoring and protecting the holy sites of Islam. Under his rule there were huge advances in culture, education, maths and science.

▲ Suleiman the Magnificent ruled from 1520 until his death in 1566.

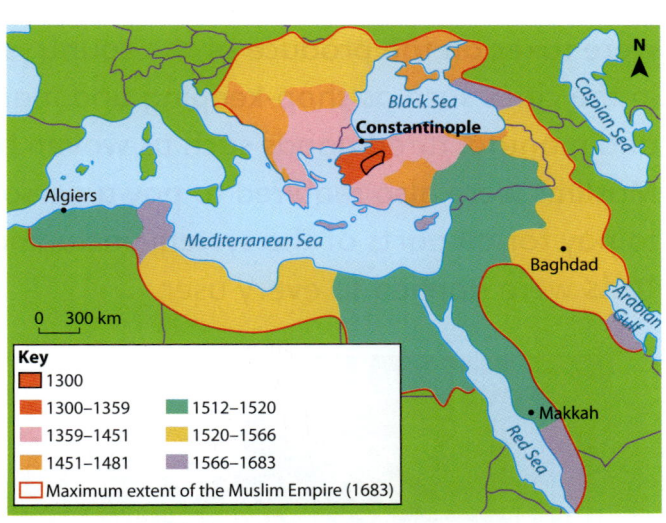

▲ The expansion of the Ottoman Empire between 1300 and 1683.

Activities

1 Draw portraits of Osman I, Mehmed II and Suleiman the Magnificent, then write a brief description of what each of these men achieved.

2 Colour a copy of the map showing lands around the Mediterranean Sea to show the areas controlled by the Ottoman Empire at its greatest extent.

2.4 Success of the Ottomans

In this lesson you will learn:
- why the Ottoman Empire was so successful
- above achievements during Ottoman rule.

Government

The Ottomans eventually ruled an empire with lands in Europe, Asia and Africa, which gave them a great deal of control over much of world trade. To control all of these lands and their trade, the Ottomans developed a very well-organised system of government.

At the top of the system were the ruler and his family. Beneath them were important officials called grand **viziers**. They controlled the army and organised the working of another layer of government in each part of the empire.

One of the main purposes of the government was to collect **taxes**. There were taxes on the produce of the countryside and the sea, and on activities in the cities such as shop-keeping and market-trading. Imports and exports and manufactured goods such as woven baskets were also taxed. Non-Muslims were also required to pay a personal tax. Taxes provided **revenue** to pay for all parts of the system, including the road network where special **tolls** were applied to every user.

▲ Trade was at the heart of the Ottoman Empire. Construction of the Grand Bazaar in Istanbul began in 1455, two years after the city was captured by Mehmet II.

If the people of a conquered territory accepted Ottoman rule they were not forced to change their culture or their way of life or their religious beliefs. The Arab nations accepted Ottoman authority because they saw them as protectors of the Islamic faith and guardians of holy sites and cities.

Ottoman culture

The 15th and 16th centuries saw great advances in all areas of life within the Ottoman Empire, again mostly paid for
by the wealth generated from taxes.

Literature developed in many forms. Poetry had been popular for a long time but even greater works were now achieved in story-writing and in works of science and mathematics. A medical atlas called 'Imperial Surgery' appeared in 1465, and there were several important works on astronomy. As the empire expanded by land and sea, geographical and historical records were kept, describing places and events in the new territories.

▲ Part of a page from a Mamluk copy of the 'Automata of al Jaziri' or the 'Book of Knowledge of Mechanical Devices'.

This period also saw great progress in the arts and crafts, such as ceramics, textile work and rug-making. Classical Ottoman music was another important part of the culture, making use of a mixture of Middle Eastern, Anatolian and Central Asian instruments.

Remarkable achievements were also made in architecture. The royal architect for 50 years was Sinan (1491–1588), who designed over 300 buildings, bridges, tombs, fountains and mosques throughout the empire.

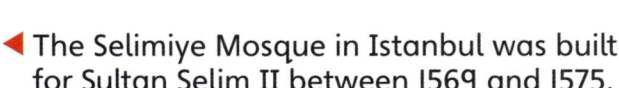

◀ The Selimiye Mosque in Istanbul was built for Sultan Selim II between 1569 and 1575.

Activity

Work in a group to prepare a presentation showing the organisation of the Ottoman Empire, and how culture and science were able to flourish.

2.5 The struggle for control

In this lesson you will learn:
- how world trade developed during the period of the Ottoman Empire
- ways in which trade and exploration are linked.

Medieval worldwide trade

Trade has always had the potential to create great wealth. The more control over a trade a person or organisation has, the more of the possible wealth they have for themselves. The control of trade has been one of the reasons for the creation of empires.

For many centuries, luxury goods, silks and spices have been traded from the lands of South-east Asia, China, India and East Africa to the markets in Europe. The Middle East region has always been at the centre of this trade.

Arab traders and sailors controlled the trade across the Indian Ocean and had built up good trade relations with their trading partners. Arab traders exchanged pearls from the Gulf and incense from Yemen and Oman for the spices and exotic materials from India and South-east Asia. They took these to the markets of Europe up the Red Sea and the Gulf or across Arab-held lands.

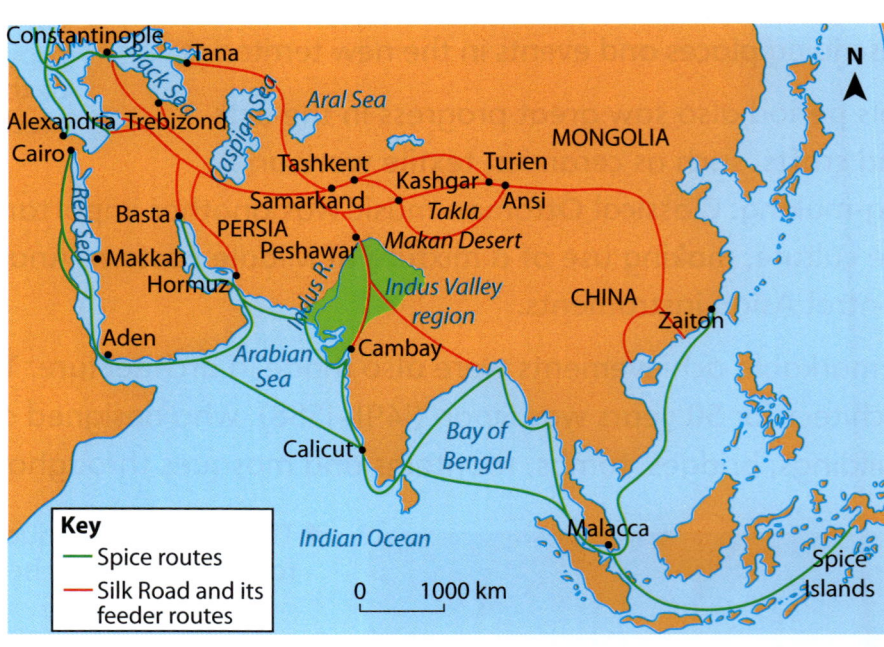

▲ The traditional routes for the spice trade were largely under Arab control.

In 1488, a Portuguese explorer called Bartholomew Dias sailed around the southern coast of Africa for the first time, proving that there was another way to reach the Indian Ocean. In 1498 Vasco da Gama followed this route and sailed to India, where he quickly realised the potential for trade and wealth. From this time the Portuguese sought to control trade across the Indian Ocean.

The Portuguese failed to take the town of Ormuz, which offered control over the Arabian Gulf, but they were successful in capturing Muscat in 1507. They gradually took control of further lands on the southern coast of the Arabian Peninsula and along the Arabian Gulf as well as in India and Africa.

▲ The Portuguese built many forts to protect their positions and their ships.

The new trade routes created by the Portuguese had a bad effect on Arab traders and on the Ottoman Empire which held lands in the Arabian Peninsula and in Egypt.

The Portuguese held control over trade in the region for almost 150 years.

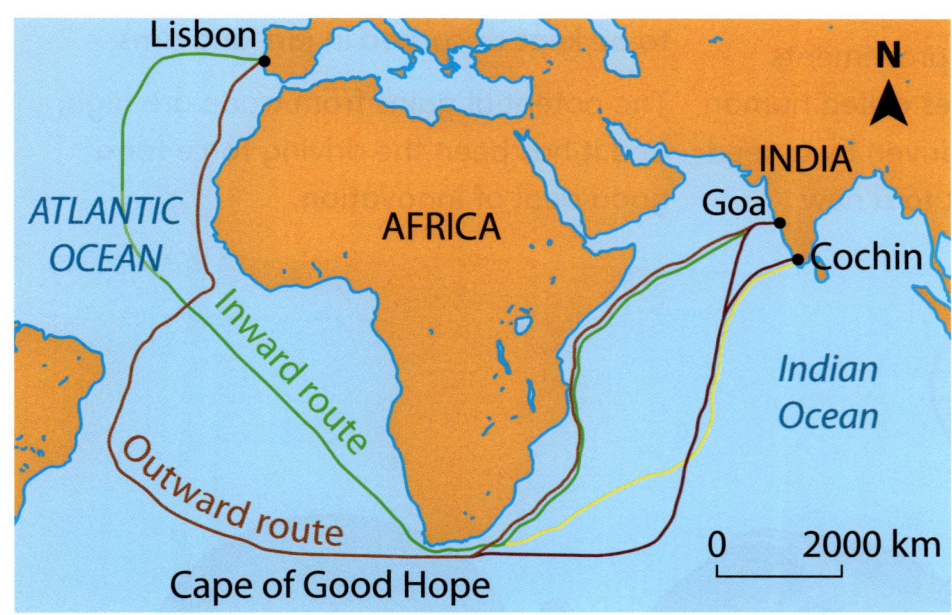

▲ The routes created by the Portuguese avoided the routes controlled by Arab traders.

Conflict and trade relations

Venice is a city located at the northern end of the Adriatic Sea. By the 1400s it was the centre of a powerful republic that was a gateway to Europe which relied heavily on trade for its wealth. As rivals to the Portuguese the Venetians maintained strong trading relationships with the Ottomans, but they were also often in conflict with them, and the two groups fought several wars.

Activity

Write a brief explanation of how the Portuguese came to dominate the trade in the Indian Ocean, and the effect this had on Arab, Ottoman and Venetian traders.

In these lessons you will learn:
- how world trade developed
- to identify ways in which trade has encouraged exploration and invention
- how things other than goods are exchanged along trade routes.

People have constantly developed and adapted the societies in which they live, seeking the means of improving the conditions in which they live and the ways in which they work.

This constant striving for improvements and innovations is sometimes called human progress. Progress is often driven by a need to solve a problem or adapt to a new situation. For example, the invention of the wheel made moving heavy or bulky objects easier. Dams and **irrigation** systems overcame water shortages in dry and arid areas. Pottery allowed produce to be kept or carried in jars and urns.

The potential gains from trade are high, and it has been the driving force for a good deal of innovation.

▲ The first wheels may have been made from mud or clay and later ones from wood.

Trade and money

Early trade simply involved exchanging one thing for another. A farmer who had grown cereals would take some of the crop to market to exchange it for things he needed, such as vegetables or clothes.

A major limitation with a system that involves simple exchange is that you only have the actual goods to trade with. If you have exchanged a sack of grain for a pile of blankets, you only have blankets to trade with. In other words you can then only trade with people who need blankets.

When money was invented it helped to solve this problem. If you brought your grain to a market and exchanged it for money (instead of blankets), you could then buy the things you needed from anyone who was selling those things, instead of only from those people who wanted your blankets. In addition, you only had to carry some coins around with you rather than of a pile of blankets.

The size and ease of use of money were advantages over actual goods. The disadvantage of money was that it was easier to lose and for other people to steal. People eventually invented the idea of a **bank**, which meant that traders were able to make money at a market in a particular place, and then deposit some of it in a local bank. They could use this money when they returned to do some more trading. In the meantime they took the actual goods they had traded back home, and got ready to supply new stock for trading at a later date.

An empire extended across a wide area but when the money was standardised across that area, then money could be used to trade anywhere within the empire.

▲ These coins were minted in the reign of Suleiman the Magnificent.

Trade and sea transport

The best way to transport goods over long distances is by sea. Early, primitive boats were cut from the trunks of trees. Other ideas included stretching a material, such as animal skin, over a framework and then applying waterproofing. The early settlers in Mesopotamia used boats made from reed bundles.

Trade required ever faster and larger ships. Shipbuilders were constantly coming up with new ideas and designs for the ship, for the sails and for ways of steering.

▲ A 9th-century Arab ship.

Trade and exploration

Navigating a ship safely across great stretches of open ocean was very difficult. Early sailors developed an amazing understanding of the movements of the sun, sea currents, wind patterns, sea colour and movements of sea life to help them establish their position by day. At night they used the stars as reference points. Mathematics and science was applied to the creation of instruments that made this easier and more accurate.

Trade and writing

Early writing was a form of keeping accounts. As agriculture developed and people settled into towns and began trading, they needed to keep a record of the exchanges that were being made. The first records that are recognised as an early form of writing come from the Sumerian civilisation in Mesopotamia in about 3000BCE. The Sumerians had libraries of clay tablets that contained their laws, literature and also business transactions.

Trade and culture

When people from one culture traded with another they exchanged things other than goods. They were also able to find out about one another's culture and way of life and their different ideas and beliefs. This exchange of ideas was revealed in many ways, including the spread of understanding about mathematics and science. Paper-making, printing, gunpowder and the compass all found their way to the western world from China along the Silk Road trade route.

Trade and faith

Trade allowed for people of different faiths to travel and meet. The extent of the Muslim Empire by 1500 shows a strong relationship with long-distance trade routes. It is possible that as Muslims came to dominate in certain areas then their trading partners would embrace Islam and so share a common culture and outlook.

◄ Early writing took the form of shapes pressed into clay.

Activity

Work in a group to make a presentation explaining the link between trade and one part of 'human progress'.

2.8 Scientists and explorers

In this lesson you will learn:
- about developments and inventions that helped exploration
- about the important contributions of some Muslim scientists and explorers in history.

Muslim explorers and sailors applied their knowledge of mathematics and **astronomy** to the problems of **navigation** at sea. Travelling over land is made easier by the use of landmarks which are features that act as a point of reference. In the middle of the sea there are no such reference points and sailors learnt to use the positions of the sun, moon and stars as a guide. Mariners' compasses and astrolabes were important instruments that were developed and improved by Muslim seamen.

Muhammad ibn Musa Al Khwarizmi

Muhammad ibn Musa Al Khwarizmi (about 780–850CE) lived during the time of the Abbasid dynasty. He was a poet, mathematician, astronomer and geographer. He brought together mathematical ideas from Ancient Greece and India and created a system of operations known as algebra.

Another of his great works was the 'Book on the Appearance of the Earth' which originally included references for lines of **latitude** and **longitude** as well as a map of the world.

▲ This statue of Muhammad ibn Musa Al Khwarizmi is in Uzbekistan.

Muhammad al Idrisi

Another important early geographer was Muhammad al Idrisi who worked in the court of King Roger of Palermo on the island of Sicily in the 1100s. Perhaps his greatest work is a map of Europe, North Africa and Asia, known as the 'Tabula Rogeriana'. This was

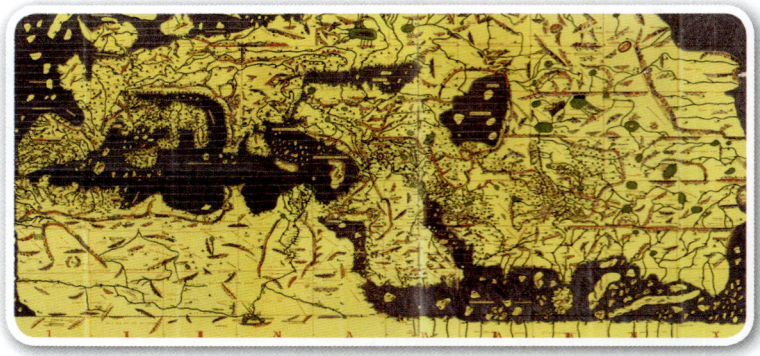

▲ A modern copy of the Tabula Rogeriana.

produced in 1154 and remained the most important geographical reference for almost 300 years.

Ibn Battuta

Ibn Battuta lived in Tangiers, a town in Morocco. In about 1325 he journeyed via Syria and Palestine to undertake the Hajj to Makkah. Rather than return home he began a life of travel which took him first to Baghdad and then to Iran, Yemen, East Africa, Oman and the Arabian Gulf. In his lifetime he journeyed throughout the Muslim world and beyond into Russia and China. He was appointed a judge in Delhi in India and in the islands of the Maldives.

Ahmad ibn Majid

Ahmad ibn Majid was born in Jalfar in present-day Ras Al-Khaimah in about 1432–37. His father and grandfather were well-known navigators, sailors and writers. Ibn Majid is said to be the person who enabled Vasco da Gama to make his journey across the Indian Ocean. He would certainly have had enough knowledge of the currents, winds and routes to allow him to offer this help. He also knew the routes of the western China Gulf and the South-east Asian seas. He recorded his knowledge in several works, the most famous of these being 'The Book of Profitable Things Concerning the First Principles and Rules of Navigation'.

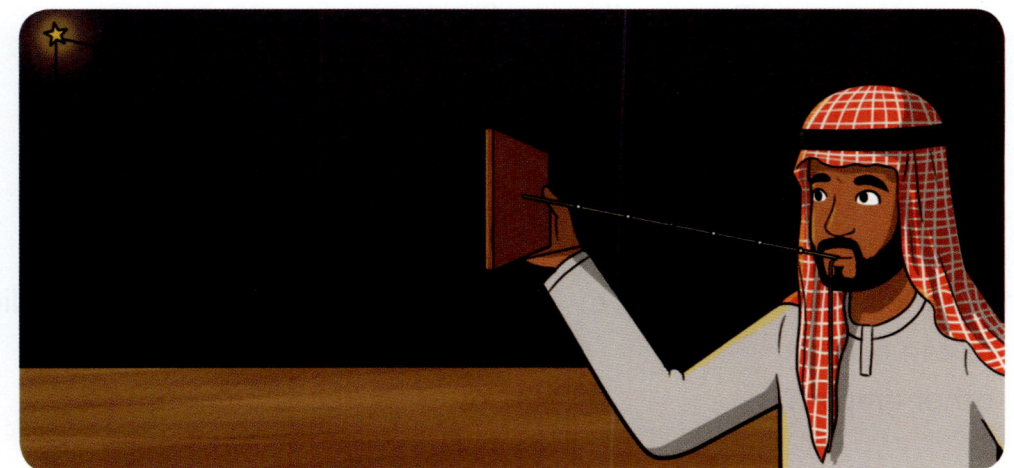

◀ Ahmad ibn Majid would have been familiar with the kamal. The kamal, meaning, 'guide', was a simple instrument used for determining latitude. It consisted of a wooden block and a knotted string which was held in the teeth.

Activity

Write a short biography to describe the achievements of one of these famous people from Islamic history.

Unit 2 Review questions

1. The eastern Roman Empire became known as the:
   a Mongol Empire
   b Sassanid Empire
   c Byzantine Empire
   d Chinese Empire

2. The Portuguese wanted to control the spice trade across:
   a the Red Sea
   b the Arabian Gulf
   c the Mediterranean
   d the Indian Ocean

3. In 1488, Bartholomew Dias was the first person to sail around the south coast of:
   a Africa
   b Italy
   c the Arabian Peninsula
   d India

4. Ibn Battuta is most famous for:
   a inventing the wheel
   b writing medical books
   c travelling around the world
   d designing buildings

Use this timeline and your knowledge of Social Studies and History to answer questions 5 and 6.

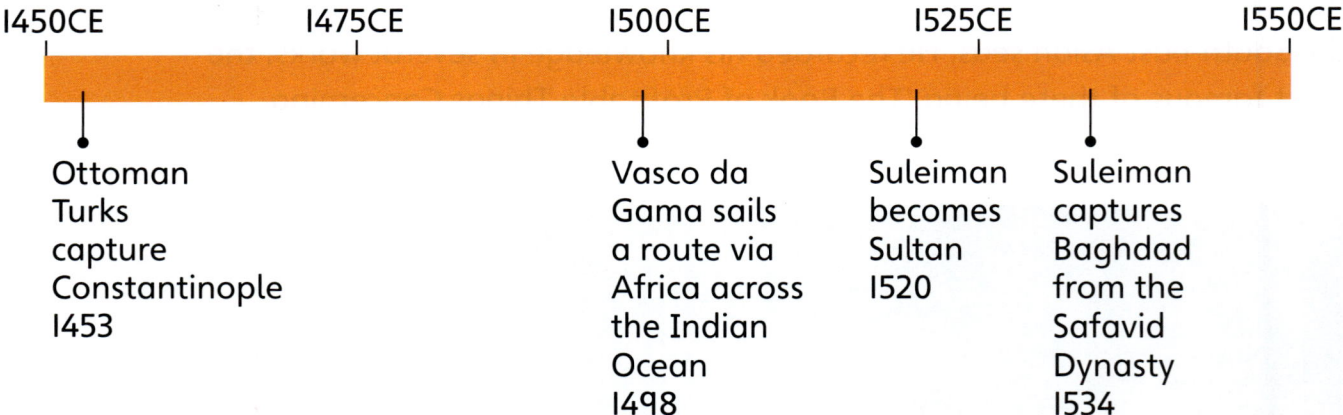

1450CE — 1475CE — 1500CE — 1525CE — 1550CE

Ottoman Turks capture Constantinople 1453

Vasco da Gama sails a route via Africa across the Indian Ocean 1498

Suleiman becomes Sultan 1520

Suleiman captures Baghdad from the Safavid Dynasty 1534

5. Which events from the timeline show that the Ottomans were in conflict with more than one other empire?

6. Which of the following statements is true?
   a The Ottoman Turks captured Baghdad before they captured Constantinople.
   b Suleiman was sultan when Constantinople was captured.
   c Vasco da Gama found a route to India before Suleiman became sultan.
   d Suleiman captured Baghdad from the Portuguese.

7. Explain how trade and the early development of writing are connected.

8. Suggest two possible consequences for a local population of the presence of merchants, traders and sailors from different places.

3 People and places

In this unit you will learn:
- to understand maps, using scale and compass directions
- to locate places using latitude and longitude
- to calculate time, using longitude
- to assess natural hazards and their effects on human activities
- to draw population graphs and charts
- about various resources and transport systems in the region
- to report findings from research.

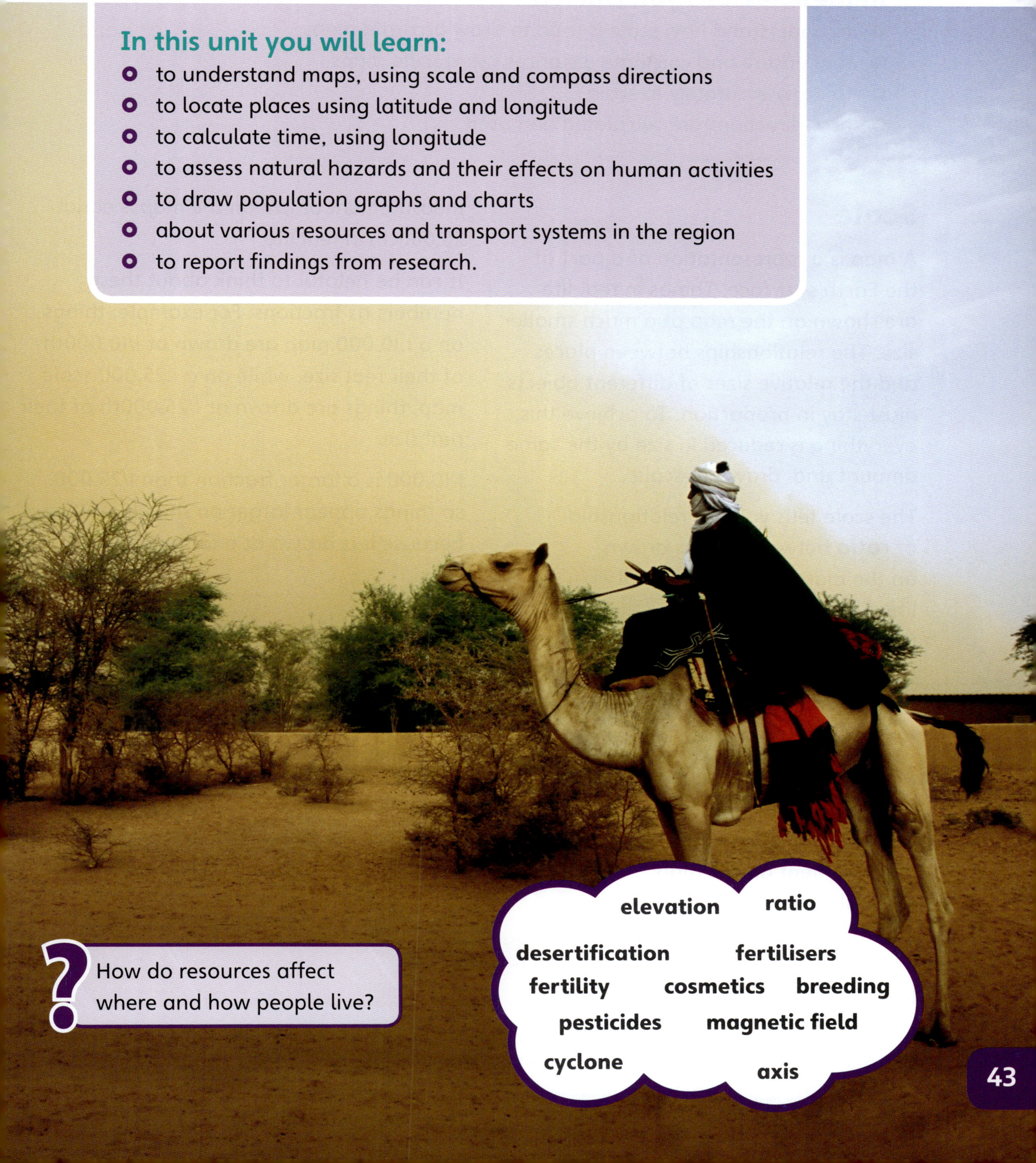

? How do resources affect where and how people live?

elevation   ratio
desertification   fertilisers
fertility   cosmetics   breeding
pesticides   magnetic field
cyclone
axis

3.1 Scale and direction

Scale

A map is a representation of a part of the Earth's surface. Things in real life are shown on the map at a much smaller size. The relationships between places and the relative sizes of different objects must stay in proportion. To achieve this, everything is reduced in size by the same amount and 'drawn to scale'.

The scale tells you the relationship or **ratio** between things drawn on the map and things in real life. The scale is not always the same, so it is important to look for a scale on a map before reading it or using it for any measurements.

A scale on a map that is given as 1:10,000 means that every single unit of measurement on the map is equal to ten thousand units in real life. So a measurement of 1cm on the map is equal to 10,000cm (or 100 metres) in real life. On a map drawn to a scale of 1:25,000, a measurement of 1cm on the map is equal 25,000cm in real life.

It can be helpful to think about these numbers as fractions. For example, things on a 1:10,000 map are drawn at 1/10,000th of their real size, while on a 1:25,000 scale map, things are drawn at 1/25,000th of their real size.

1/10,000 is a larger fraction than 1/25,000, so things appear larger on the 1:10,000 map because it is drawn at a larger scale.

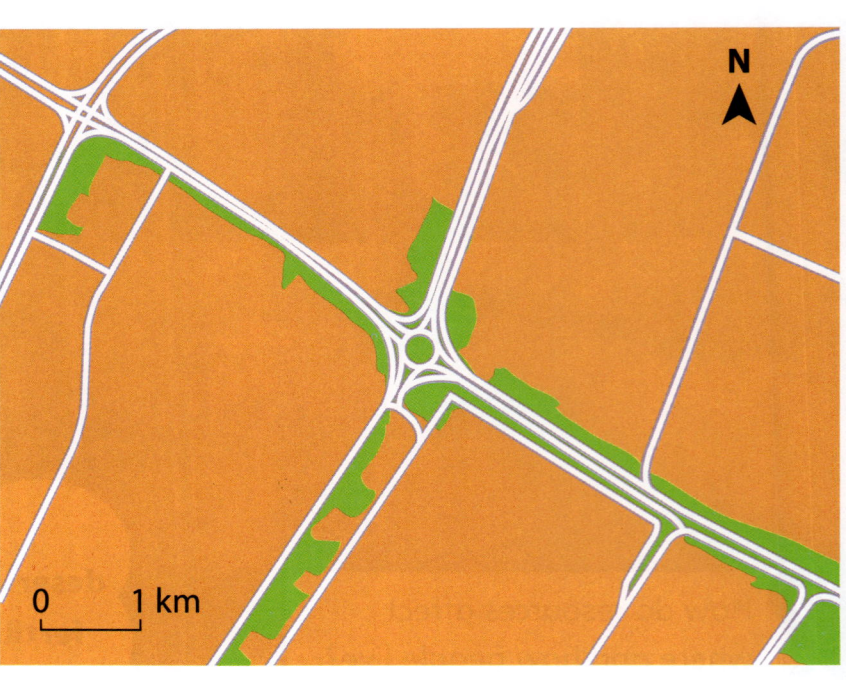

▲ A map drawn at a smaller scale covers a wider area but shows less detail.

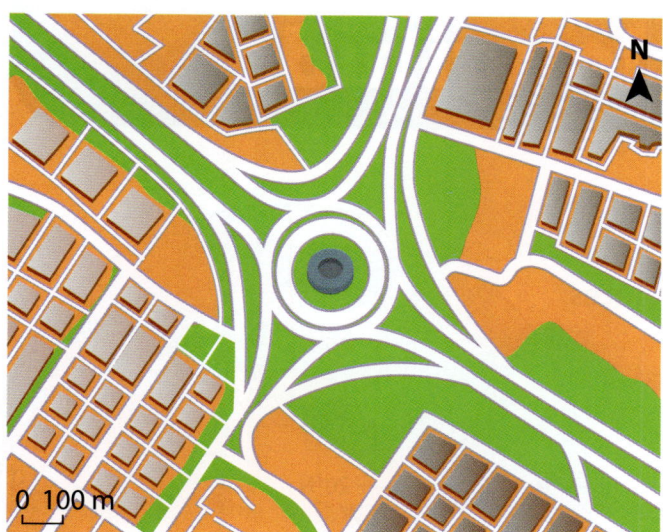

▲ A map drawn at a larger scale shows more detail but covers a smaller area.

A compass works because the Earth produces natural **magnetic fields** which have two poles: a north pole and a south pole. The 'south' pole of the compass needle is attracted to the north pole of the Earth's magnetic field, so it always spins to point towards the north. The compass is then turned so that the direction showing north on the instrument lines up with the direction in which the needle is pointing. All the directions can then be read off from this.

Drawing to scale

Drawing to scale uses the same idea of ratio. If you use a scale of 1:2000, every centimetre on your drawing is equal to 2000cm, or 20 metres, in real life. On a drawing of 1:50,000, every centimetre on the drawing is equal to 50,000cm, or 500 metres, in real life.

Compass directions

A compass is a special instrument for showing and measuring direction. The face of a compass shows different compass points. It also has a magnetic pointer, called a needle, which can rotate freely around the centre.

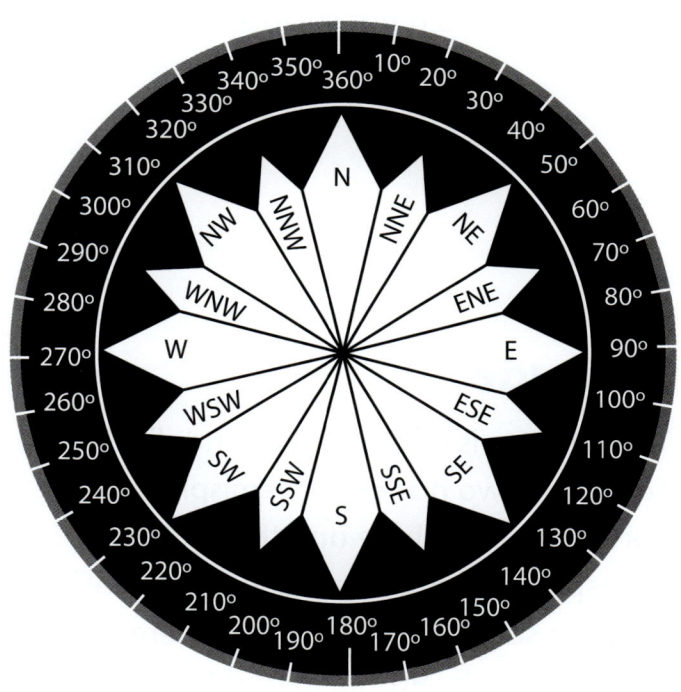

▲ A compass is based on a circle and the different directions are shown around the circle. Positions are measured in degrees, so compass directions are given as degrees from North (or 0°).

Activities

1 Practise measuring the distance between two locations on a map.

2 Draw a scale plan of your desk with some objects on it.

3 Draw a scale plan of your classroom.

3.2 Latitude and longitude

In this lesson you will learn:
- about latitude and longitude
- to use latitude and longitude to locate places.

To help people identify locations on the Earth, people use globes and map projections or maps. A globe is a scale model of the Earth. A map projection is the surface of the globe 'projected' onto a flat surface.

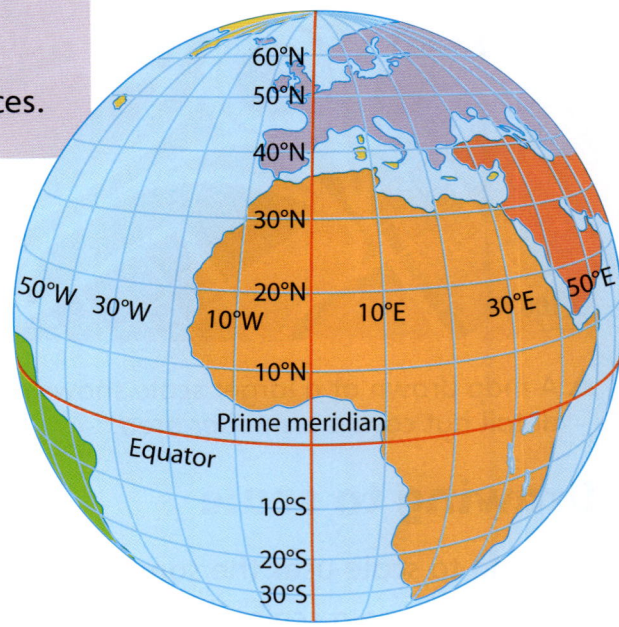

▲ We use a set of imaginary lines to help us identify a location or position on the Earth.

Latitude

The equator is at 0° latitude and divides the Earth into two halves or 'hemispheres': the northern hemisphere and the southern hemisphere. Lines of latitude give a position north or south of the equator. There are 180° of latitude: 90°north and 90° south.

▲ Lines of latitude are at certain degrees from the line of the equator. Do you notice anything about the lines of latitude?

Longitude

Lines of longitude give us a position east or west of the Prime Meridian, or 0° longitude. This is a line of longitude that runs through Greenwich in England. Lines of longitude all

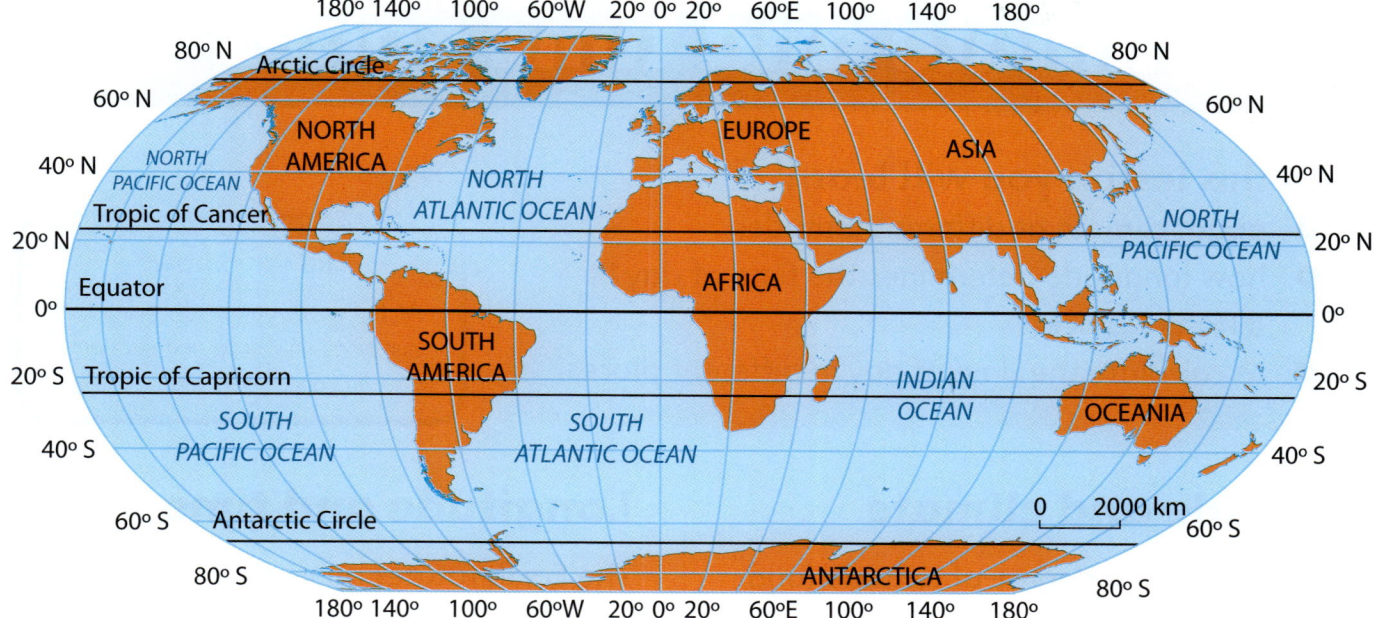

▲ World map showing lines of latitude and longitude.

run through both the north and the south poles. There are 360° of longitude
and they divide the lines of latitude into 1° segments.

Finding a location

To identify a location on the globe we need to know its degree of latitude
and of longitude. If a map only shows lines of latitude and longitude at set
intervals, for example every 10°, it is necessary to estimate where a value that
falls within this interval would be. For example, a latitude of 35°N would be
halfway between latitude 30°N and 40°N. A longitude of 127°W will be just over
halfway between longitude 120°W and 130°W.

When identifying a location it is customary to give the latitude first, for example
26°N, 43°E.

Activities

1 Draw a map showing lines of latitude at intervals of 15°.

2 Name the continents that these lines of latitude pass through:
   0° (the equator), 20°S, 60°N, 20°N.

3 Name the continents that these lines of longitude pass through:
   0°, 60°E, 60°W, 120°W.

4 Work out the latitude and longitude of your present location. Write down two
   countries on the same latitude as yours, and two on the same longitude.

3.3 Climate and time zones

In this lesson you will learn:
- about climate at different latitudes
- how longitude determines the time of day in different places
- to calculate the time of day in different places.

Latitude and climate

In general, as the degree of latitude (and therefore the distance from the equator) increases, the average temperature slowly decreases. This is explained in Figure A below.

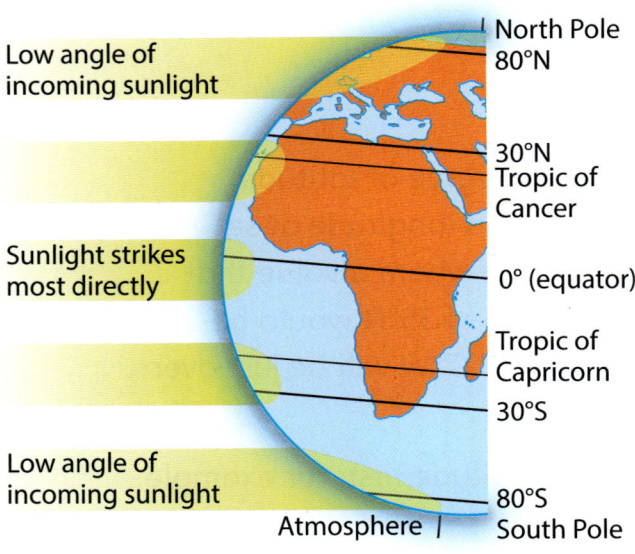

Low angle of incoming sunlight

North Pole
80°N

30°N
Tropic of Cancer

Sunlight strikes most directly

0° (equator)

Tropic of Capricorn

30°S

Low angle of incoming sunlight

80°S
South Pole

Atmosphere

▲ **A** The sun's rays are more intense at the equator. They are spread out over a wider area and must travel through a greater volume of the atmosphere at higher latitudes.

The climate zone immediately north and south of the equator is tropical. The tropical zone (sometimes called 'the Tropics') lies approximately between latitudes 23.5°N (called the Tropic of Cancer) and 23.5°S (the Tropic of Capricorn).

Other significant lines of latitude are known as the Arctic Circle and the Antarctic Circle.

Longitude and time

The Earth rotates on its **axis** in an anti-clockwise direction, once every 24 hours. This spinning is what causes us to experience day and night. The Earth turns through 15° of longitude every hour. This is calculated by dividing 360 by 24.

The time of day in any one place is determined by the longitude of that place. If we know the time difference between two places at any one time and the longitude of one of them, we can work out the longitude of the other place.

N

15°

12

11

10

9

8

7

6

S

▲ **B** Longitude determines time of day or night.

In Figure B, the line of longitude at the shadow line is the point at which the sun 'rises', shown here as approximately 7.30am.

At every 15° of longitude east of that point it is an hour earlier. The longitude where the time shown is 10am experienced sunrise approximately two and a half hours earlier. At the longitude where it is shown as being 12 noon, the sun will be at its highest point in the sky.

The Prime Meridian at Greenwich is at 0° longitude. If, as in Figure C, it is 6am in Greenwich and 9am at a second location, we know that the second place is at 45°E because each hour difference is 15° of longitude and 15 x 3 = 45. We know that it is 45°E and not 45°W because the Earth rotates in an anti-clockwise direction, so the place where it is later in the day will have seen the sunrise earlier.

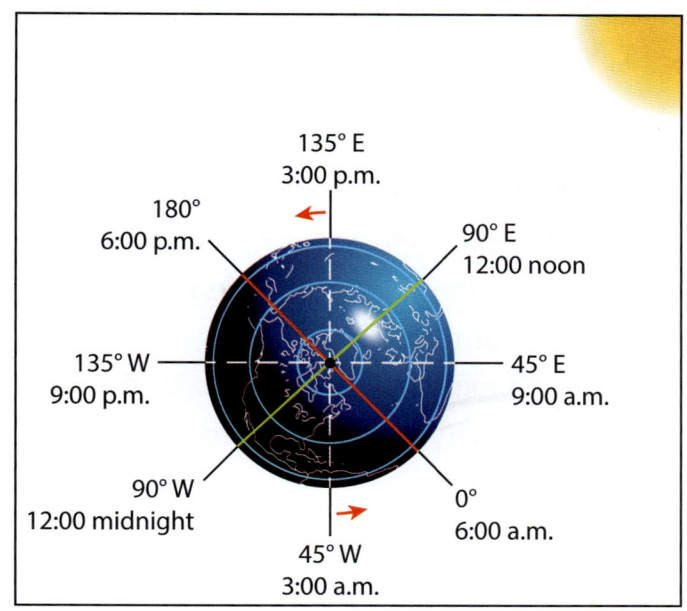

▲ C This view of Earth, looking down from above the north pole, indicates the different times of day, determined by longitude, when it is 12 noon at longitude 90°E.

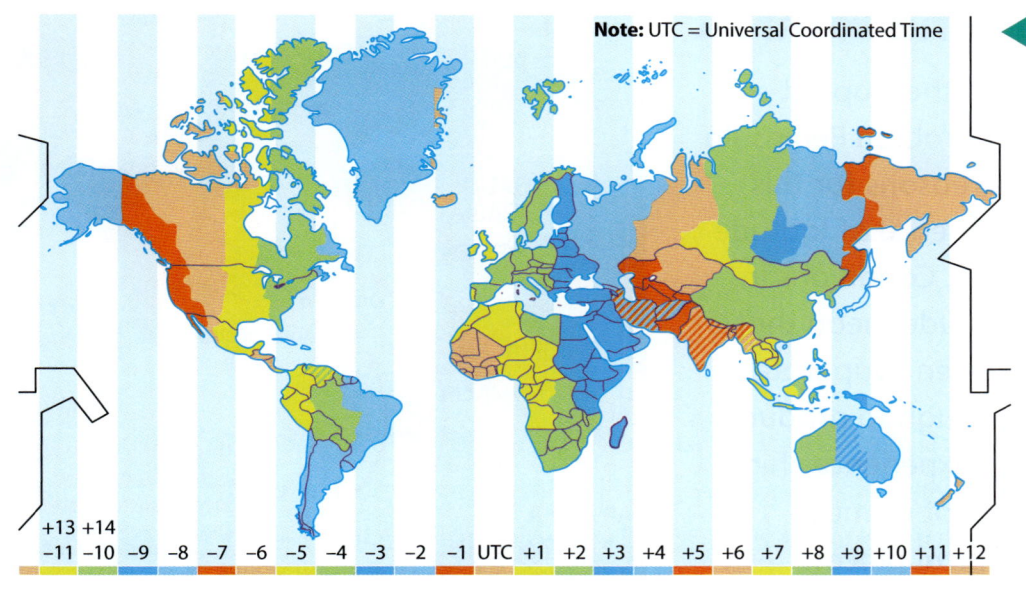

Note: UTC = Universal Coordinated Time

◄ D The world's time zones. Each 15° of longitude creates one time zone. For geographical and political reasons, the actual times used in some countries do not always correspond to the longitude.

+13 +14
−11 −10 −9 −8 −7 −6 −5 −4 −3 −2 −1 UTC +1 +2 +3 +4 +5 +6 +7 +8 +9 +10 +11 +12

Activities

1 Draw a simple diagram to show the world's different climate zones. Identify the approximate latitudes for their boundaries.

2 Write down the time where you are now, and what the time is in five different places around the world. Do this by calculating the difference in longitude and then compare this to the actual time used according to the world's time zones.

3.4 Climate and human activity

In this lesson you will learn:
- to describe the climate of the Arabian Gulf countries
- to identify weather features of the Arabian Gulf countries
- to explain how climate and weather affect human activity in the Arabian Gulf countries.

Factors influencing climate

The main influences on the climate of an area are latitude, ocean currents, wind and **elevation**. Other factors influence the climatic conditions experienced in a particular location.

Latitude, winds and rainfall

Despite being partly within the tropical climate zone, most of the Arabian Peninsula has a desert climate. The reasons for this are quite complex. The influence of latitude here is on rainfall and wind. Conditions in the atmosphere at this latitude mean that any clouds that do form often evaporate before they grow large enough to produce rain. The region therefore experiences high tropical temperatures but not as much rainfall as some other tropical places.

However, areas at this latitude and in this region also experience 'monsoon winds' which do bring rain to parts of the peninsula.

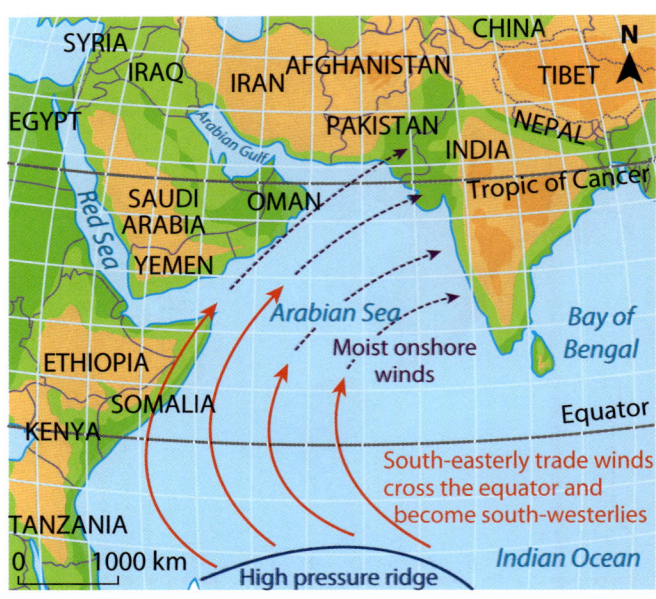

▲ Although the region spans the Tropic of Cancer, the climate of the coastal areas of Saudi Arabia, Yemen, Oman and the Arabian Gulf countries is described as sub-tropical and dry.

Relief and climate

Warm air picks up water vapour as it travels over water. The air moves up when it meets high ground and it cools down. Cooler air cannot hold as much water vapour and this turns into water droplets in a process called condensation. The water droplets fall as rain over the higher ground.

Higher levels of rainfall in parts of the Arabian Peninsula are largely due to the presence of mountains and the influence of monsoon winds that blow from the south-west during the period from late May to September. Low clouds and light rain are common features during this time.

Land masses and bodies of water

When air passes over water, it picks up moisture. Clouds form and eventually these may produce rain. The Arabian Peninsula is located between the two vast land masses of Africa and Asia, so the air arriving in the region is largely dry.

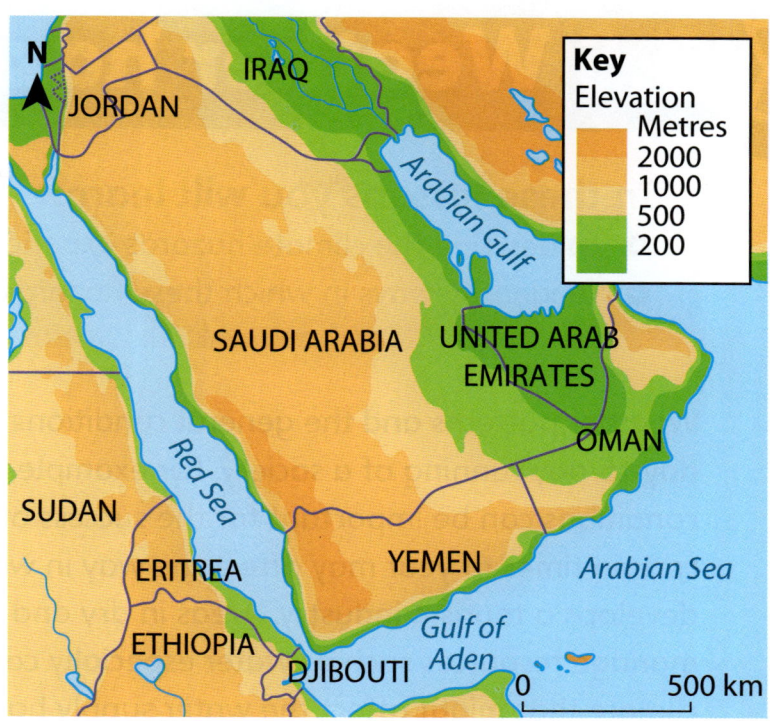

▲ Elevation has an impact on climate and weather conditions.

Humidity is a measurement of the amount of moisture in the air. A high level of humidity can sometimes mean that there is a greater chance of rain. This also affects how well people are able to control their body temperature, because sweat does not evaporate so quickly in humid conditions. This means it can feel uncomfortable in the high humidity experienced in a number of coastal regions around the Arabian Peninsula.

Effects of climate on human activity

Human populations need to have sufficient food and water resources to survive. The climate affects how much of these resources are readily available, and also where people can live. In modern societies, because of transport and other advances in technology, people can live further away from these essential natural resources.

Activity

Write a brief report describing the climate and weather features of the Arabian Gulf countries. Explain their effects on human activity.

3.5 Weather hazards 1

In these lessons you will learn:
- to describe the climate hazards experienced in the Arabian Gulf countries
- to identify ways in which these hazards affect human health and activity.

Weather patterns and the general conditions of the climate affect the day-to-day running of a society. For example, the regularity of certain conditions can be important for the success of agriculture. Conditions at certain times of year may affect the way in which an area or region develops a tourism industry. Areas in dry and arid climate zones have to manage resources such as water especially carefully, and changes to the climate that might affect the water supply have to be taken very seriously.

▲ Agriculture relies on regular and predictable climate and environmental conditions.

People can only survive in a certain range of temperatures and they suffer in extremes of heat or cold. If the climate of a region is generally close to one of these extremes, then a change in the climate that might make it warmer or colder is a matter of serious concern.

In countries of the Arabian Gulf, in addition to concern over general trends such as these, there are also particular climate-related events that present hazards to human health and safety.

Extreme temperatures

Extremely high temperatures pose a threat, as people can suffer from dehydration and heat exhaustion and even die. In the Arabian Gulf countries the generally high temperatures result in a high demand for electrical power to run air-conditioning units.

▲ An extreme event in 2010 saw the temperatures in Jeddah, Saudi Arabia, reach 52°C. The demand for power forced eight power plants to close.

Sand and dust storms

For up to three months in late spring and early summer, the strong north-westerly 'Shamal' wind blows almost constantly. This wind travels from Turkey across Jordan and Syria collecting dust and sand along the way. It moves down the Arabian Gulf towards the United Arab Emirates before turning inland to the Rub Al Khali desert. The wind can create dust or sandstorms that may reduce visibility to just a few metres. Strong winds can also blow in the winter months. Although these last for a shorter time they also create sand and dust storms.

A dust storm can tower into the sky and be several thousand metres thick. This has a serious impact on air transport and can result in airports being closed. Land transport, and the shipping and fishing industries, can also be affected. If visibility is reduced to a few metres then driving, in particular, becomes very dangerous.

Everyday human activity is also interrupted because it is unpleasant to be out in a dust storm. For some people the dust can cause problems with breathing and damage to the eyes.

◄ Sand and dust storms create a number of hazards for human life and activity.

Drought

Drought is defined as a prolonged period of time during which there is less than average rainfall or even no rainfall at all. It is one of the worst climate hazards and worldwide it has been responsible for millions of deaths and huge amounts of environmental damage. Areas that are normally able to produce crops or sustain livestock are not able to do so during a drought, so agricultural productivity decreases. If people are not able to get the food they need in order to survive they abandon the area where they live and move elsewhere.

The Arabian Peninsula has limited water supplies and so is vulnerable to a climate hazard such as drought. People need water to drink but fresh water is also needed to maintain agricultural industries which provide not only food but also employment.

Flash floods

Flash floods are caused when there is an excessive amount of rain over a short period of time. Flash floods are often caused by rain falling in mountain areas. Torrents of water then pour down wadis, sometimes breaking over their banks. In city areas they flood streets and cause damage to buildings, bridges and trees as well as being a threat to life.

▲ Flash floods threaten life and property.

Tropical storms and storm surges

A tropical **cyclone** is large rotating storm system. They usually form over large bodies of warm water and feature very strong winds, thunderstorms and heavy rain. Each year there is a season during which these tropical storms can begin over the Indian Ocean. Tropical storm events are not common in Arabian Gulf countries but they do occur.

Cyclone Gonu formed during the cyclone season of 2007 off the south-west coast of India and began heading in the direction of the Arabian Peninsula. It became steadily larger and stronger as it crossed the ocean but had begun to weaken by the time it reached Oman. Even so, the winds were still very strong at about 100km/hr. They knocked out power and telephone lines in many places, including Muscat. Much of the coastline was damaged, along with buildings and roads in the towns. Fifty people were killed. The storm moved on to the United Arab Emirates where it caused huge waves to overwhelm coastal areas around Fujairah, flooding roads and destroying several fishing boats.

◀ Tropical storms have a great deal of power and can cause a lot of damage.

Activities

1 Prepare a written report or presentation that describes the climate and extreme weather hazards that can affect the countries of the Arabian Gulf. Your report should also explain how these hazards affect human health and activity.

2 Work in a group to research recent climate-related events that have presented hazards to human health or prevented human activity in an Arabian Gulf country.

3.7 Population

In this lesson you will learn:

- why populations are counted
- to describe features of the populations of the Arabian Gulf countries
- to interpret and present population information in different charts and diagrams.

Population characteristics

Populations have different characteristics, such as sex or gender structure, which has to do with the different numbers of males and females, and age structure, which describes the different numbers of people of various ages.

Knowing this kind of information helps determine where resources need to be allocated. For example, older people need healthcare and younger people need educational facilities. The sex structure can suggest, for example, the number of places needed at different educational establishments and the types of health services required, such as maternity care.

The age structure also affects the number of people who are said to be of 'working age'. This includes everybody who is neither too young nor too old to be working.

Population pyramids

A special chart known as a population pyramid is often used to show the age structure of a population for both males and females.

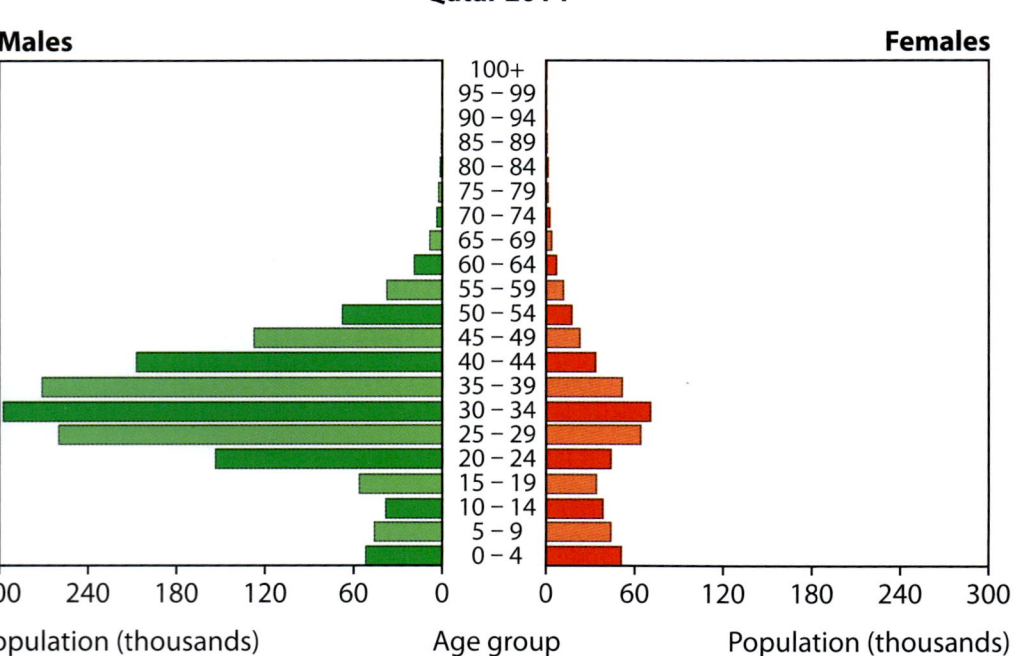

◀ A population pyramid for Qatar.

Qatar 2014

Males — Females

Population (thousands) — Age group — Population (thousands)

Pie charts

Pie charts are used to present different types of information. They are divided into sectors to show the size of particular amounts in relation to the whole. When used for population information the circle represents the whole population and the sectors are different groups within that population.

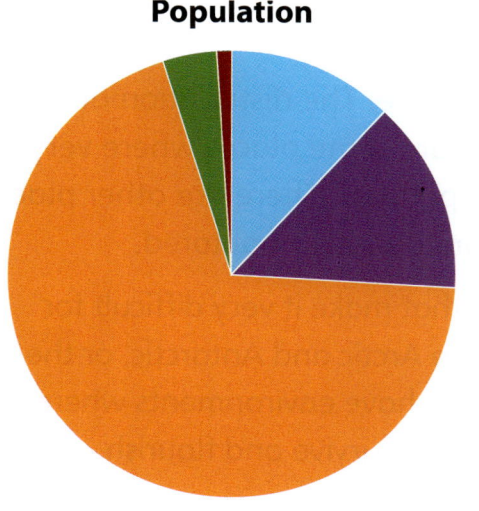

Population

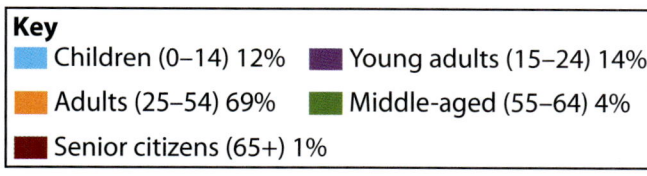

Key
- Children (0–14) 12%
- Young adults (15–24) 14%
- Adults (25–54) 69%
- Middle-aged (55–64) 4%
- Senior citizens (65+) 1%

▲ A pie chart showing different population age groups as percentages.

Making a pie chart using percentages

To draw a pie chart, you need to represent each part of the data as a proportion of 360, because there are 360 degrees in a circle. You need to calculate the number of degrees in the angle for each sector. Assuming that you have a set of percentage figures that add up to 100%, first take the percentage of one sector and write it as a decimal (for example 19% is 19/100 which equals 0.19, 25% is 25/100 which equals 0.25, 8% is 8/100 which equals 0.08.etc.). Multiply this decimal number by 360 to find the angle measurement for each sector of the circle (for example 0.19 x 360 = 68°).

Bar charts and line graphs

Bar charts and line graphs are useful for showing other types of population information, for example changes over time.

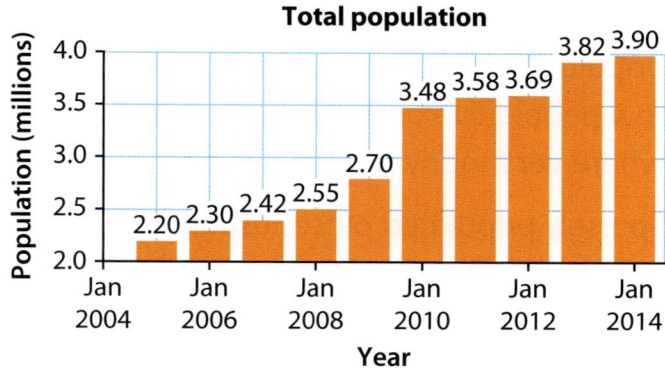

Total population

▲ This bar chart shows how a population changes over time.

Activities

1 Use the percentage figures shown in the pie chart above to create your own accurate copy of that diagram.

2 Find out how the population of your country has changed in the last ten years. Draw a bar chart to show this.

3 Write about what the government might do based on the information in your chart.

3.8 Population distribution

In this lesson you will learn:
- that populations are not evenly spread
- to explain why people live in particular places
- how population information can be shown on maps
- about urbanisation.

Population distribution

Population distribution is the pattern of where people live. The distribution of populations is not even. Throughout the world there are some places where very few people live and we say that they are sparsely populated. There are other places where very many people live and we say that they are densely populated.

Sparsely populated places usually have environments that make it very difficult for people to live there, for example the frozen areas of the Arctic and Antarctic, or the hot, dry areas such as deserts. Densely populated places have environments where it is easy for people to live and they can get all they need to survive and flourish.

Population density

Population density is a measurement of the number of people living in an area. It is calculated on the basis of a particular measurement, such as a square kilometre (km^2). It is an average number and so it does not always reflect exactly the situation in real life. So, for example, an area of 100 km^2 might have a population of 50,000. The population density would be: $50,000 \div 100 = 500$ persons per km^2

If you measured the actual population of each square kilometre you might find that there were more than 500 people in some and fewer than 500 in others. Over the whole 100 km^2, the population would still be 50,000 and the average population 500/km^2.

Maps showing population density are shaded to show areas of different density.

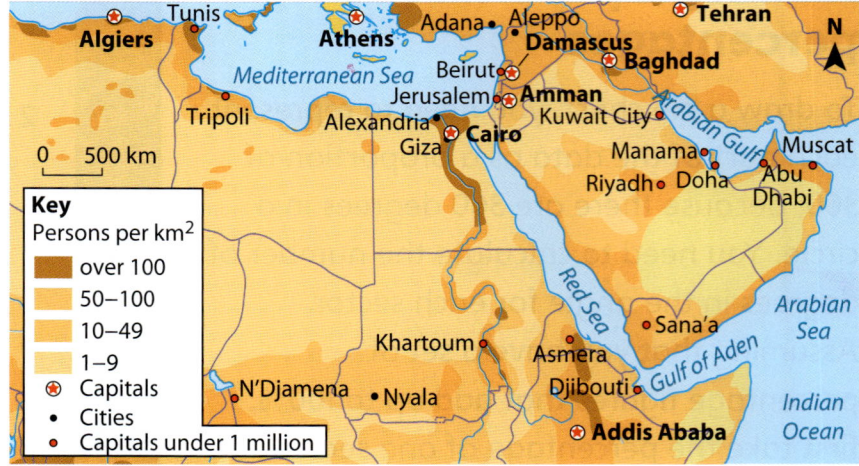

▲ Population densities across the Middle East and part of North Africa.

Urbanisation

Urbanisation is a word used to describe the way in which more people are choosing to live in cities, or urban areas, rather than in the countryside, or rural areas.

For most of world history, more people have lived in rural areas than in the towns. This was partly because agriculture, which had to feed the whole population, took place in these rural areas. Agriculture also needed a lot of workers. In more recent times, agricultural machines have replaced workers and so there are fewer jobs in rural areas. Agriculture is hard work and many people feel there are more opportunities in cities.

▲ Today it is estimated that more people in the world live in towns and cities than in the countryside.

Country	Percentage of the population living in cities and towns
Kuwait	98
Saudi Arabia	82
Bahrain	89
Qatar	99
United Arab Emirates	85
Oman	73

▲ The percentage of people living in urban areas in the Arabian Gulf is very high.

Activities

1 Research the population distribution in your country. Then write a brief explanation of this pattern of distribution.

2 Find the information you need to calculate the population density of your country, or of a city within it.

In these lessons you will learn:
- about resources available from agriculture and fisheries.

The importance of food production

A population has to feed itself. Instead of growing the food they need for themselves, most people today rely on agriculture to provide it. As populations increase in size, the amount of food agriculture and fisheries need to produce also increases. When a country's agricultural and fishing industries cannot meet the demands of the population, food has to be imported from other countries. The extent to which a country can feed itself is known as its level of food security.

Arabian Gulf countries face two challenges. Firstly, the populations in the region have increased dramatically in the last half-century. Secondly, the environmental conditions make it difficult to produce greater amounts of food, and fish resources are almost all fully exploited. Increasing output is very difficult.

The Arabian Gulf countries have the challenge of feeding their growing populations. This is also a worldwide issue. The population of the planet in 1959 was about 3 billion. This had doubled in 40 years to reach 6 billion by 1999. In 2013 there were estimated to be 7 billion people on Earth. Estimates suggest that this growth will continue and that by 2050 the population will have grown to 9 billion.

To feed this population, some experts estimate that world food production will need to increase by 70%.

◀ Countries of the Arabian Gulf import a lot of food. One problem with importing food is that its price can change very quickly. If there is a worldwide shortage of a particular food, then it becomes much more expensive.

Changes in farming

Agriculture has gone through many changes, from traditional activities using simple tools and animal herding through to the highly developed practices that can be found today. New technologies and developments in plant **breeding** and cultivation are always being introduced as countries attempt to provide more of the food their populations need.

Scientists study plants and seek to develop varieties that are able to survive in different conditions. They also study the different soils to see which will be good for growing crops.

Hydroponics

Hydroponics is a method of growing plants without using soil. Plants can be grown with just their roots in water which has plant nutrients dissolved in it. This way of growing crops is used in a number of countries in the Arabian Gulf. The amount of water used can be very carefully controlled, which avoids waste. In addition, the amount of water needed is much less than in traditional methods, sometimes using up to 70% less. Furthermore, any water that is not used by the plants or has not evaporated into the air can be captured, filtered and recycled.

▲ In hydroponic systems plants are often grown in large greenhouses in which conditions such as temperature are also carefully controlled in order to create ideal growing conditions. The land where these greenhouses are situated does not need to be suitable for agricultural purposes.

Agricultural produce

Farmers in many Arabian Gulf countries are being encouraged to grow a wider range of crops. This is partly because when there is a large supply of one type of product, the prices go down, so each farmer has to sell more to make the same amount of money. It is also not a good idea to depend too much on a single crop in case there is a disease or another problem that causes a crop to fail.

In addition, if farmers are able to grow more of the crops that people want then these will not have to be imported from other countries.

▲ Agricultural produce from Arabian Gulf countries.

Vegetables and salads	Fruits	Cereals and fodder crops	Cash crops	Animal products
celery, potatoes, cucumbers, lettuce, peppers, tomatoes, cabbage, red cabbage, cauliflowers, carrots, beans	citrus fruits, mangoes, melons, dates	wheat, alfalfa	roses, chrysanthemums	meat, eggs, milk

Fisheries

Marine and fisheries resources include pearls which were once the main part of the economy for some countries. Today, fish is a popular part of people's diet and fishing is a popular form of recreation.

The fishing industry has faced a growing demand for its products from a rapidly increasing population. There is concern about the sustainability of these fisheries because over-fishing has reduced the fish stocks and habitats have been damaged by the impact of urban and industrial development.

Important habitats for fish and marine life include the places where they breed as well as the areas where they live when fully grown. The coastal wetlands and mangrove swamps and the sea-grass beds in some countries of the Arabian Gulf are important fish 'nursery grounds'.

◀ Marine environments are also a resource because they can act as tourist attractions.

> **Did you know?**
>
> According to EWS-WWF (an environmental group), the level of grouper fish, which includes the very popular hamour, dropped by between 87% and 92% between 1978 and 2003, due to coastal development and unsustainable fishing.

Activities

1 Find out about some types of agricultural production in your country. Identify the products, how and where they are produced and what they are used for.

2 Write a letter to a government minister asking for funds for a hydroponics farm you hope to set up. Your letter should explain briefly how the system works and the advantages you think it has to offer. Also explain how it will help with your country's food security.

3 Find out about some of the fish species caught in the Arabian Gulf and the Gulf of Oman.

4 Design a poster that encourages people to choose to buy fish from sustainable sources.

3.11 Oil, gas and minerals

In this lesson you will learn:
- about oil, gas and mineral resources.

Oil and gas

Oil is made from the long dead remains of plants and animals. Crude oil is a thick, black liquid found underground which is converted in oil refineries into a range of different fuels. These have different names and uses. Perhaps the most familiar form is petrol or gasoline. This, along with diesel, is used for fuel in cars and other forms of transportation. Other fuel products include kerosene, aviation fuel and liquefied petroleum gas (LPG).

Oil products are used to make many other things including **cosmetics**, medicines, paints and lubricants.

Natural gas is found near oil under the ground. It is pumped out and sent along pipes to storage facilities. Natural gas is then sent to people's homes to be used for cooking and heating. It is also sent to power plants to create electricity and to some factories that use a lot of energy, such as aluminium refineries.

▲ As well as earning money for the country through sales of oil and gas, the oil industry provides employment opportunities for many people.

Bauxite

Bauxite is an ore which produces a material called alumina. This is used to produce aluminium in a process that requires a lot of energy. The Arabian Gulf countries are well supplied with energy resources and so aluminium smelting is an important part of the economy for some of them. Saudi Arabia has large supplies of bauxite and there are aluminium refineries there and in other countries including Bahrain and the United Arab Emirates. Bauxite is also imported from other countries and the processed aluminium is exported.

▲ Minerals are often processed and refined to produce other materials.

Fluorite

Fluorite is a mineral with several uses. In some forms it can be used to create items of jewellery. In other forms it is used in different processes such as aluminium refining and producing glass. There are deposits of fluorite in Kuwait.

▲ Some minerals such as fluorite can look very beautiful and can be made into jewellery.

Other minerals

Small amounts of other minerals are found in various countries of the Arabian Gulf region. These include chromite, limestone, copper, gold, iron, gypsum, sand and gravel.

Activities

1 Mark on a map the location of oil and gas fields and refineries in the Arabian Gulf countries.

2 Carry out some research into some regional mineral resources and the ways in which they are used.

3 Write a brief explanation of the benefits of oil, gas and other mineral resources to the Arabian Gulf countries.

3.12 Land and its uses

In this lesson you will learn:
- about the competition for different uses of land
- to identify the environmental concerns connected to different land uses.

Land as a resource

Roughly 71% of the Earth's surface is covered with water, which leaves 29% of the surface made up of land. The land surfaces of the planet have to accommodate all people and allow for all the activities that must take place in order for human life to continue. Conditions in the environment, such as the climate or the terrain, mean that some areas are not suitable for human habitation. This means that the amount of land surface that is suitable for providing all our needs is even less than 29% of the planet's surface.

Agricultural land use

It is estimated that over 40% of the Earth's land surface is currently used for agriculture. We face the challenge of feeding an ever-growing global population.

Agriculture must produce more food but agricultural practices must also be sustainable. This means that they are carried out in such a way that they do not destroy the environment and especially the soil.

▲ In many parts of the world, forest is cleared to grow food or cash crops.

Land used for agriculture is often cleared of natural vegetation which provides the habitat for many different types of plants and animals and so must not be completely destroyed. Areas of woodland and forest also play an important role in regulating the climate of the whole planet.

Modern agriculture uses chemicals such as **pesticides** and fertilisers. These can affect the natural balance of an environment and can be a direct health threat if they get into water supplies.

Soil erosion is the movement of soil by water, wind and gravity. Some agricultural practices can speed up the process and in extreme cases lead to a process called **desertification**. This is the process in which once-productive land becomes less productive. The soil loses its **fertility** and water passes through the soil more quickly. This makes it difficult for plants to grow. Since plant roots hold soil together, if they are not present the soil is more likely to move.

◀ Tree planting is an effective way of combating desertification.

Other land uses

Land is in demand for housing because shelter is another of our basic human needs. Land is also needed for all the other activities that make up modern life today – for places of work and education, for factories and power plants, for areas of rest and relaxation and for all the transportation systems that link these different parts together.

Activities

1 Carry out research and produce a report on the competing land uses in your area.

2 Write a letter to a company asking for funding to buy tree saplings for a tree planting programme to combat desertification. Describe the problem you are trying to address and explain why planting trees will help.

3.13 Regional transportation

In this lesson you will learn:
- about the different transportation systems in the region.

Transport networks make many other parts of modern life possible. In the past, people had to be close to the resources they needed, to the place where they worked and to the markets for the things they made. Today, people, resources and manufactured goods travel large distances using various forms of transport.

Public and private transport

Private transport is anything that is owned by an individual or company for private use, including cars, commercial vehicles, planes and boats. Public transport is transport that is used by members of the public, including aircraft, buses, trams, monorails, railways, ferries and water taxis.

Transport networks

Transport can be considered at four levels:

1 Local transport, meeting the needs of a neighbourhood or a city

2 National transport, allowing for travel within a country

3 Regional transport, connecting different countries within a region

4 International transport, connecting different countries around the world

Different transport networks connect together to make up the whole system. People and goods coming from another country usually arrive at a large site, such as an airport or a seaport. Hundreds of people can arrive in a single aeroplane and thousands of tonnes of goods can be transported in an ocean-going vessel. From these points of arrival they must travel to other places. A national network lets people and goods reach different parts of a country, and a local network allows them to reach their final destination.

Local transport

A local transport network connects neighbourhoods or places across a city such as homes, schools, factories and office blocks. Vehicles using the local network are limited in size and the important feature of the system is the flexibility and range of options it offers.

▲ A metro system is unaffected by traffic on the local road network.

▲ Developing the region's road network is a major part of future development strategies.

National transport

The national or 'domestic' transport network moves people and goods between cities and other places within a country. A national system can include roads, railways and airports.

Regional transport

Regional transport networks are an important part of co-operation between the countries of a region. In the Arabian Gulf, the regional transport network includes road, sea and air transport and there are proposals for a railway that will link all the countries together.

A regional transport network is especially important in terms of trade between neighbouring countries and with those across a wider area.

International transport

International transport has become increasingly important. Goods and passengers can arrive by sea or by air. The airports and seaports where they arrive are major developments.

Activity

Work in a group to prepare a brief report on either local or regional transport networks. Your report should explain how the different elements are important to the economy.

Use this map and your existing knowledge to answer questions I, 2 and 3.

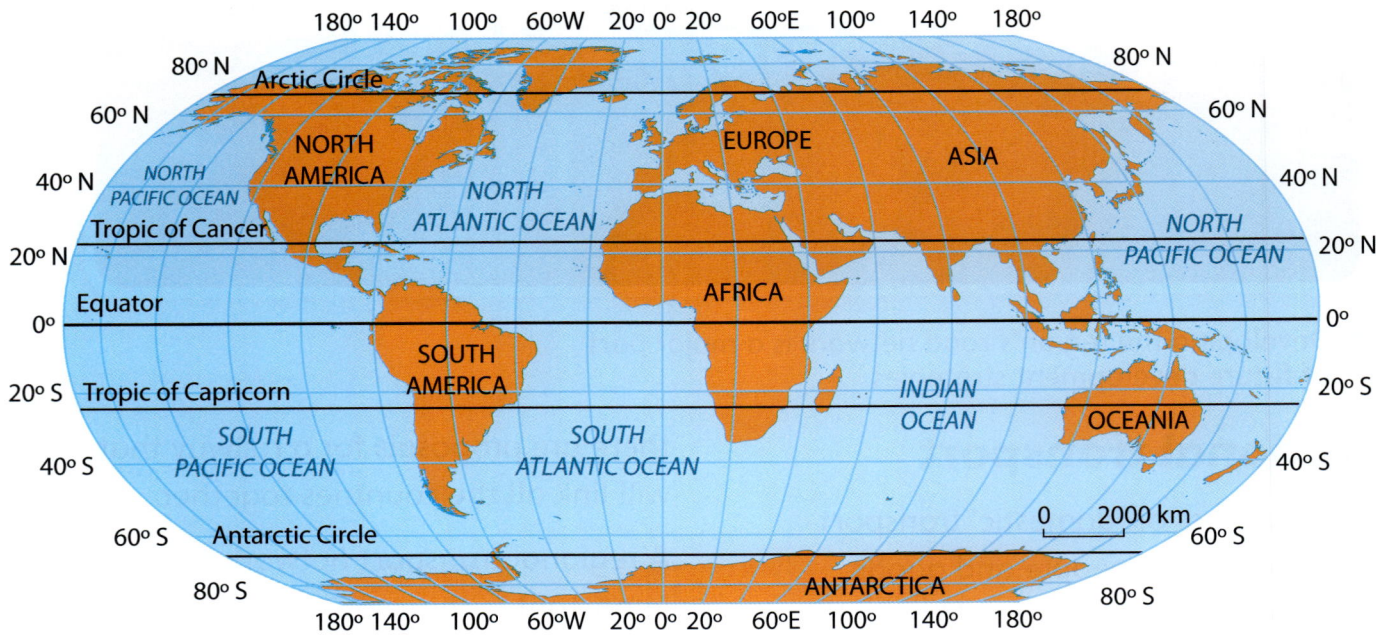

I   Name two continents that lie on latitude 20°N.

2   Name two continents through which longitude 40°E passes.

3   Copy the true statement:
    a   The Arabian Peninsula is in the northern hemisphere.
    b   The Arabian Peninsula is in the southern hemisphere.

4   The time is different in different places on the Earth by one hour for every:
    a   10° of longitude
    b   12° of longitude
    c   15° of longitude
    d   20° of longitude

Use this population pyramid and your knowledge of Social Studies and Geography to answer questions 5 and 6.

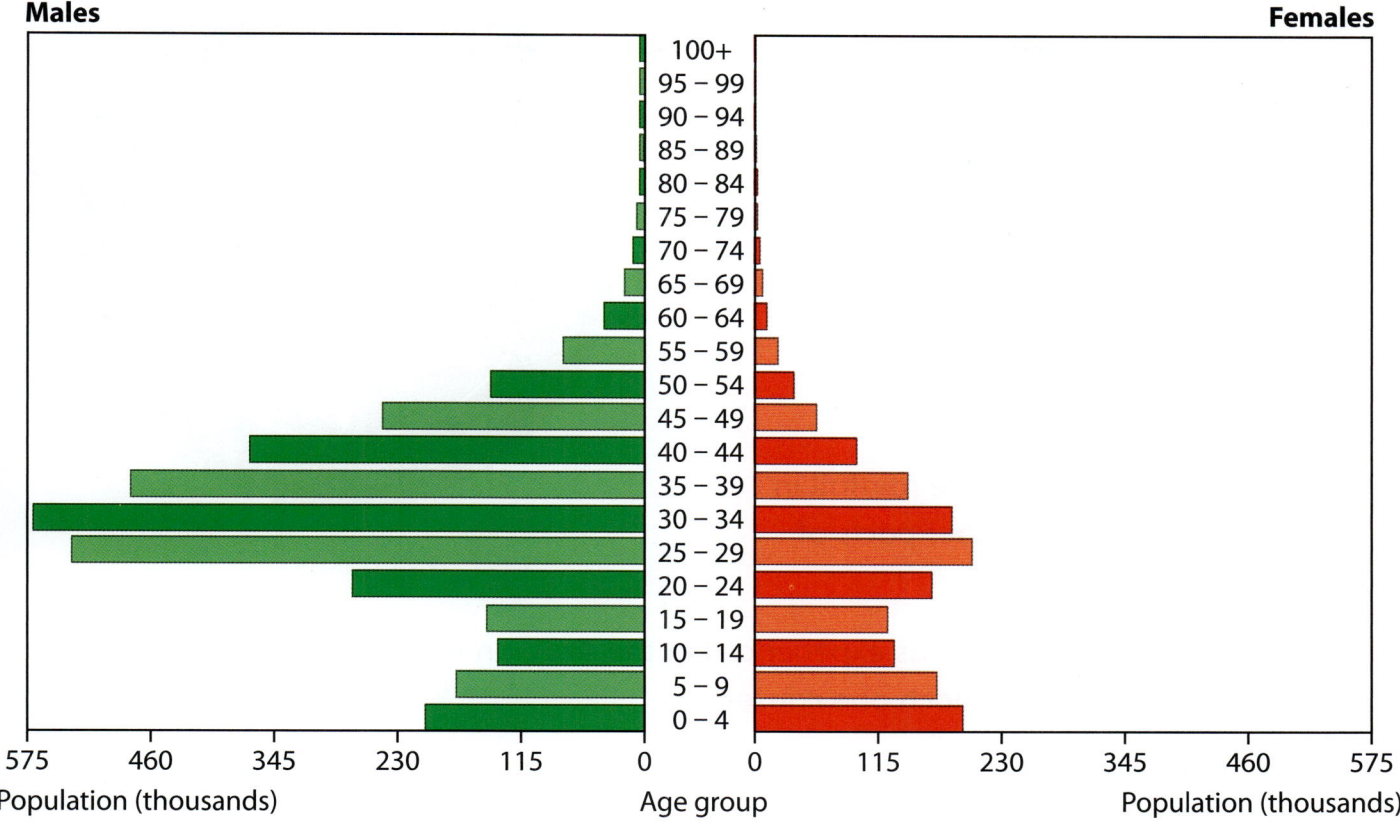

Males

Females

Population (thousands)

Age group

Population (thousands)

5   Which of the following statements is true?
   a   The age group with the smallest number of people is 60–64 year olds.
   b   There are more males aged 20–24 than females.
   c   There are more women aged 50–54 than men of the same age.
   d   People under the age of 20 make up the largest part of the population.

6   The population pyramid shows that there are more males than females in this country. What might be the cause of this situation?

7 I am looking north-east and turn clockwise by 90°. Now I am facing:

    a north

    b south-east

    c east-south-east

    d east

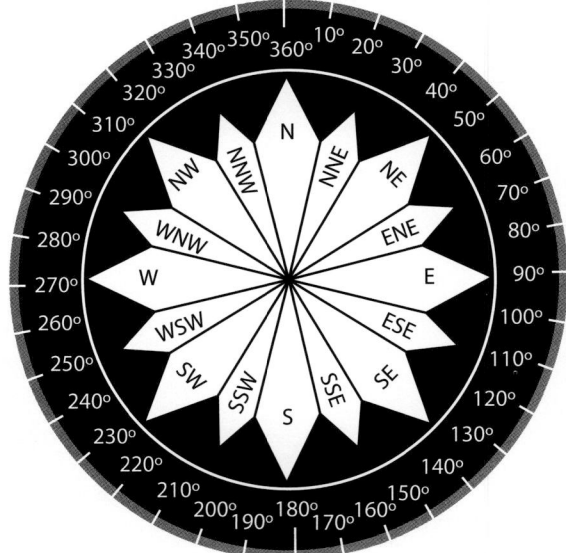

8 My compass shows I am facing 292.5°. I am facing:

    a west

    b north-west

    c west-north-west

    d west-south-west

9 Explain why there is more rainfall in Oman than in some other parts of the Arabian Peninsula.

10 Name two weather hazards experienced in the Arabian Peninsula. Describe the problems each one causes.

11 Write about three agricultural crops that are important in the countries of the Arabian Gulf.

12 Describe two ways in which land can be used as a resource.

4 Citizenship

In this unit you will learn:
- to work together to create a useful society
- that we all have rights and responsibilities
- ways in which we should care for the environment
- to role play a public meeting
- to evaluate and analyse the mass media
- about the meaning and consequences of consumerism and materialism, and why people work
- about the structure and functions of a country's government
- how countries in the region work together.

? What different reasons might people have for going shopping?

charity   bloc
federation   monopoly
head of state
social media   ministry
election   policies   duty
lobby   tax   vote

4.1 A united nation

Patriotism

People can have very strong positive feelings about their country, perhaps because it is beautiful or because it offers a good experience of life. If they also feel a strong commitment to that country and want to do what they can to help it improve, then we say they are patriotic.

If a person trains hard and finally wins a medal, or works hard in class and makes good progress, he or she has a right to feel proud. Patriotism is about having positive feelings towards a country. It is to do with feeling proud of the good things achieved by your country and the progress made in different areas of life.

Patriotism is normally associated with people who are born in a country and who recognise it as their 'home'. For these people there can be a natural sense of belonging and a desire to help the country be the best it can be.

▲ Many countries hold national festivities simply to celebrate their existence and their achievements.

The populations of many countries today include people who have chosen to live in a country that is not their country of birth. These people may think about another country as being their home but it is still possible for them to feel proud of the country in which they live and for them to want to see that place be the best that it can be.

These feelings mean that all people in a population can decide to make a positive contribution to society.

Being part of a society

Many countries today have a multicultural society which is made up of people from different backgrounds and cultures. One challenge for these kinds of society is preserving the country's own culture while enabling people both to make a positive contribution and to celebrate and enjoy their own culture.

One way of doing this is to identify all the parts of life that people have in common. Regardless of their differences, all people want a country to be the best that it can be. They can care about the feelings and rights of other members of a society and share a concern for people's safety and wellbeing. All people want the available resources to be used wisely for the benefit of everyone.

▲ We can help the environment in many ways wherever we are.

Activities

1 Write a list of the shared values and goals that you think would help people in a country live and work well together.

2 Work in a group to make a list of ways in which people can work together to make your country a better place to live.

4.2 Active citizens

In these lessons you will learn:
- to identify ways in which citizens can have an active role in society
- to think about how pressure groups operate in society.

There are many opportunities for citizens to have an active role in society. Citizens need to know something about the government, how it works and the influence they can have. They should know about the community in which they live and take an active role there too.

Charity

Charity is not a new idea. There seems to be a part of most people that feels a desire to offer help in different situations. When we think about offering help to other people it is usually because we see that they are in need and are not in a position to meet that need themselves. Today there are also charities concerned with protecting wildlife and the environment.

▲ Charity can include giving money to help people.

Volunteering

A volunteer is somebody who agrees to do something without expecting any material reward in return. People often volunteer to work on behalf of a charity or not-for-profit organisations. These organisations need to keep their costs down because they want all the money they have available to go towards the cause they are supporting. When people volunteer then the organisation does not have to pay wages to staff to get the work done.

People can volunteer on a regular basis where there is a continuous need, or they can volunteer to help out with special events.

Community groups

Many people join community-based organisations, help to run community events and offer help to people who need assistance. There are many opportunities to help the natural environment and to improve society or the lives of certain people. This can be achieved simply by visiting people who are unwell or in hospital, or by spending time with people who are lonely.

◄ Volunteering helps to build a stronger, better community. There are many ways in which children and young people can take part.

Pressure groups

Pressure groups exist to inform people of particular situations and to influence public opinion and government or business **policies**. A pressure group might attempt to ban advertising to children, to correct some form of injustice, or to highlight the need to protect a sensitive part of the environment.

Pressure groups can run campaigns to educate the public or offer educational materials to schools and colleges. They can also **lobby** the government so that decisions are made and policies are created that are in favour of the ideas behind the pressure group. For example, an environmental group might make the case for protecting the natural environment in a situation where there is a need for the construction of new buildings or infrastructure.

Activities

1 Find out about the volunteering opportunities available in your area.

2 Identify and discuss a situation in your area where change could lead to an improvement. Decide, as a pressure group, what you might do to bring this change about.

4.3 Responsibilities of citizens

In this lesson you will learn:
- to identify the responsibilities people have towards their country and the region.

Regional citizens

Countries within the same geographical area often have similar characteristics. They are usually within a similar climate zone and have the same types of geographical feature. These factors result in countries having similar resources and producing similar goods. In some situations the countries also share a similar culture and this can be a cause for greater unity.

▲ Countries of the Arabian Gulf share similar cultures.

In the case of the Arabian Gulf, the countries have similar experiences in recent history, with rapid development since the discovery of oil. They also face many similar challenges, such as the dry climate and the scarcity of fresh water supplies. They also share a common Arab culture and a common faith.

Responsibilities and rights of regional citizens

The responsibilities and rights of citizens of a country are much the same when applied to the region. The expectations on behaviour will be largely the same, as will the attitude towards human rights. Governments of countries in a region often co-operate in certain ways, and there is an expectation that citizens will understand and share in this co-operation.

The use of resources can also be a regional issue. For example, there may be a regional shortage of a vital resource, such as water.

Consumers

The population of a region creates a greater market than that of a single country. Today people can choose to buy products from all over the world. If people within a region choose to buy goods and services from regional producers and providers they will help these businesses to grow and become strong. If regional businesses are successful they can invest more money in continuing to make improvements to the things they offer and to the way they work.

Having a wide range of regional businesses is good, because it means a country does not become too dependent on one particular product. Governments of the Arabian Gulf countries want to encourage different businesses because they recognise that at present there is a great dependence on oil and gas.

Informed citizens

Regional citizens should have an understanding of the relationships that exist between the countries of the region, and the steps that have been taken towards greater co-operation.

▲ Buying from local or regional producers helps regional businesses to survive and grow.

▲ People are kept informed of current affairs by mass media such as newspapers and television.

Activities

1   Make a list of products available to buy which are made locally or within the region, and another list of products that are imported.

2   Find out about some important events in a country in the Arabian Gulf other than the one in which you live.

4.4 Human rights

In this lesson you will learn:
- about human rights
- about human rights in the Arabian Gulf countries.

Human rights

Human rights ensure that every person receives the things that it is felt are essential for people to live, to develop and to make the most of their potential. They are called human rights because it is understood that each person is entitled to these simply because they are human.

The basic rights address needs such as food, clothes and water. A basic human right would be that everyone should have access to clean, safe water.

Universal human rights

The United Nations is an organisation made up of representatives of countries from around the world, including Kuwait, Bahrain, Saudi Arabia, Qatar, United Arab Emirates and Oman. In 1948, the United Nations prepared a special piece of international law called the Universal Declaration of Human Rights. This document sets out the rights that all members of the UN agree should apply to all people.

▲ It is universally agreed that everyone has the right to a basic primary education.

The Arab League

The Arab League is a regional organisation of Arab countries from North Africa, the Horn of Africa and South-west Asia. The Council of the Arab League adopted the Arab Charter on Human Rights in 2004.

Human rights in Islam

The Cairo Declaration of Human Rights in Islam is a human rights declaration from members of the Organisation of Islamic Co-operation. It sets out the Islamic perspective on human rights. Among other things, this declaration states that:

- all people are equal in terms of basic human dignity, basic obligations and responsibilities, without any discrimination

- the right to life is guaranteed to all people

- everyone has the right to be safe from bodily harm

- in the case of armed conflict it is prohibited to cut down trees, destroy crops or livestock, to destroy the enemy's civilian buildings and installations by shelling or by any other means

- everyone is entitled to human sanctity and the protection of one's good name and honour during one's life and following one's death

- the seeking of knowledge is an obligation and provision of education is a duty of the state and society

- everyone has the right to the freedom of movement – this means that a person can choose to live in different parts of a country or in another country

- no one can be arrested or have his or her movements restricted unless he or she has done something wrong

- everyone has a right to freedom of expression which means that people can give their opinions as long as this is not contrary to the principles of Sharia

- people are born free and no one has the right to enslave, humiliate, oppress or exploit them.

▲ Adequate healthcare is another human right.

Activity

Make a poster promoting one of the rights from the Cairo Declaration of Human Rights in Islam.

4.5 Environmental issues

Awareness of environmental issues

We are probably most aware of damage to the environment when we experience it directly in our local area. If an area is untidy or dirty then it is not attractive to look at and it is unpleasant to live in. If an area is polluted in another way we may also be able to see visible signs of this, or there may be unpleasant smells. Some causes of **pollution** can also have a bad effect on our health, especially if they are experienced over a long period.

Pollution and damage to the environment are important issues wherever they occur because we all live in the much larger environment of the world. We need to be concerned about the environment on a regional and global scale because, even if we do not experience things directly, changes in the world's environments do have an impact on all our lives.

▲ The air is polluted by fumes from motor vehicles.

Did you know?

In 2012, for the first time, over 60 million cars were produced in a single year – that is more than 165,000 every day. It is estimated that there are over 1 billion cars on the world's streets and roads.

Human activity and the environment

Almost every human activity has an effect on the natural environment.

We create a built environment of housing, schools, commercial buildings, transport networks and other infrastructures. To do this we have to clear away some part of the natural landscape. We obtain large amounts of resources from mines and quarries for construction materials, which also changes the natural landscape.

To feed ourselves we take land and put it to agricultural use, removing natural vegetation, and then use large amounts of water for irrigation and to give to animals.

Creating all the items that we make, which we hope will make our lives more comfortable or enjoyable, uses up resources and creates pollution.

Moving around using means of transport, and many other activities, uses energy and produces various forms of pollution.

Environmental issues facing the region

In recent times the Arabian Gulf countries have all experienced very rapid growth in the oil and gas industries. The resulting rapid rise in population has led to a massive increase in the construction of housing, commercial buildings and infrastructure. The agricultural industry must produce more food, which means further pressure on the natural environment.

Environmental problems facing the region also include the decline in air quality, pollution of the marine environment and the reduction of available water resources. Different environments in the region are affected by many factors but some are especially sensitive, including the deserts, coral reefs and coastal mangrove wetlands.

▲ Coastal developments are popular because they offer wonderful views but they can also threaten delicate natural environments.

Activity

Act out a public meeting where a developer is proposing a new hotel development in a coastal area of mangrove, which will attract tourists, bring jobs and create wealth.

4 Citizenship

83

4.6 Environmental development

In this lesson you will learn:

- about government agencies created to protect the environment
- about areas of focus for government agencies
- about sustainable development.

Government environmental agencies

Governments usually have a ministry or department that is directly responsible for the environment. Other departments will be required to take environmental issues into account when considering their own areas of responsibility. For example, a ministry responsible for agriculture and fisheries will be mainly responsible for ensuring that these industries produce food but must also ensure that agricultural or fishing practices cause minimum harm to the environment.

▲ All human activities have an impact on the environment and so they must be controlled.

Non-government organisations (NGOs)

Non-government organisations (NGOs) are organisations that are not organised or run by governments. They may be able to seek funding from governments and can also ask for donations from other organisations or individuals. Some of these organisations exist to protect or preserve the environment or a particular part of it.

Regional and wider bodies

A number of bodies exist to promote environmental issues in the region and to enhance co-operation and co-ordination among different organisations. These include:

- the Council of Human and Environmental Affairs, which seeks to create a regional strategy for environmental protection

- the Council of Arab Ministers Responsible for the Environment (CAMRE)
- the Joint Committee on Environment and Development in the Arab Region (JCEDAR).

In 1991 CAMRE adopted the Arab Declaration on Environment and Development and Future Prospects. This set out principles and directives for the protection and improvement of the region's environment.

Sustainable development

Sustainable development is development that meets present needs without compromising the ability of future generations to meet their own needs.

As a country develops, there tend to be greater pressures on the natural environment. Sustainable development seeks to bring the benefits of development while limiting the negative environmental impacts. Development is not sustainable if resources are used up too quickly or natural environments are damaged beyond repair.

▲ Renewable energy such as solar power is an important part of sustainable development.

Major challenges faced by Arab countries are addressed in the Sustainable Development Initiative in the Arab Region (SDIAR).

Marine environments

Marine environments are of concern to all Arabian Gulf countries because they offer such a valuable and varied resource. Regional initiatives concerning the marine environment include the Regional Organisation for the Protection of the Marine Environment and the Convention for Co-operation on Protection of the Marine Environment from Pollution.

Conservation

The Arabian Gulf region has several very special environments that provide the natural habitats of many species of plants and animals. The deserts and marine environments, including coral reefs, seagrass beds and mangrove swamps, all need special protection.

Activity

Work in a group to prepare a presentation explaining the threats to a particular environment. Describe what is being done by the agencies involved in its protection.

4.7 Mass media

Mass media

Mass media includes any medium that people or organisations can use to communicate with a large number of people over a wide area.

Because they reach large numbers of people, the mass media can have a powerful influence. Partly for this reason, there are rules and regulations about how they operate and what is allowed to be reported. For example, there are laws that forbid the mass media from reporting things about people that are untrue.

▲ Thousands of papers are printed and sold every day.

Regional reporting

Through reporting on regional matters, the mass media can play a role in helping countries of a region come together in a closer union. Media transmissions and printed publications can help citizens to find out about many aspects of life in different countries throughout a region. By increasing this kind of knowledge and understanding, people can feel a greater sense of having a common identity.

Traditional forms of mass media

Traditional forms of printed mass media are newspapers and magazines. Traditional forms of broadcast mass media are television and radio. Broadcast media have an advantage over the print media because they can report news events very soon after they have happened or even as they are developing.

New forms of mass media

Technology, especially the internet, has completely changed the way the world communicates. Almost anyone, from individuals to large organisations, can create content and share content with other people through the internet.

These changes have brought many benefits, such as the ability for people in dangerous or remote situations to inform others of what is happening. Pressure groups and charities are also able to make use of **social media** to promote their causes.

▲ Technology means that people can be in constant and almost instant contact with the world.

Because people can share thoughts, ideas and information easily, it becomes more difficult to control what is written, said or shown. People should be free to express their opinions, unless they are unhelpful, hateful or untrue.

Ownership

Mass media organisations can be owned and operated by governments or by private companies.

Activities

1 Work in a group to carry out a survey of items in the printed and broadcast media that are about regional issues or about a country other than the one in which you live.

2 Write about the ways in which mass media can inform and influence people on regional issues such as water usage, waste disposal or the environment.

4.8 Consumerism

In these lessons you will learn:
- about consumerism and materialism
- to consider the values behind consumerism and materialism
- to consider how you are a consumer
- to consider how the advertising industry operates
- to analyse advertisements in terms of the values they represent and the methods of persuasion they employ.

Consumers and consumer goods

People who buy and use goods and services are called consumers. The everyday items that people purchase, such as food, cars, clothes and jewellery, are called 'consumer goods'.

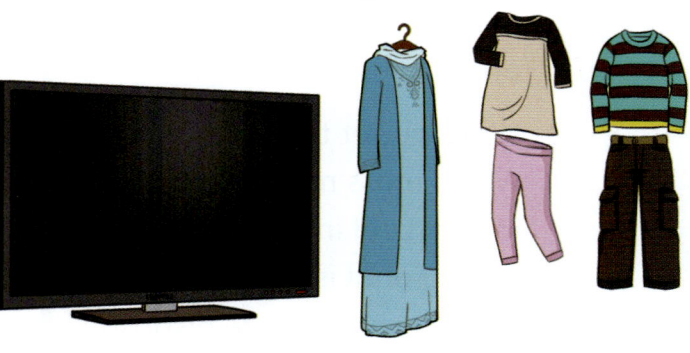

▲ Consumer goods are everyday items that people buy and use.

Consumerism

A hundred years ago, most people bought only the things they needed. By the 1950s, people in industrialised societies were being encouraged to buy more of the things they simply wanted. 'Consumerism' describes the practice of buying more and more consumer goods.

▲ Shopping for consumer goods is a popular leisure activity for many people.

Materialism

Materialism is a way of thinking and living that gives a great deal of importance to material objects and comfort. People who are materialistic are said to give greater importance to material possessions and physical comfort than to other values, and also to feel that their happiness in some way depends on the amount of material possessions they have.

Values in society

Traditional values have often stressed hard work, self-restraint and **thrift**. Some people argue that consumerism and materialism promote a different set of values, and that these may be in opposition to some accepted traditional values within Arab societies.

Children as consumers

Many children have their own money to spend. As potential consumers they are an important part of the 'market' for people who have things to sell. Children need to learn skills to make informed decisions about what they buy.

Advertising

People need to market the products and services they offer. Part of this is done through advertising. Advertisers say that what they are doing is informing potential customers of the availability of a product or service, and explaining why it is better than alternative products.

Some people suggest that advertising makes people want more than they actually need, and that it creates feelings of dissatisfaction in people if they do not possess a particular product or item.

As people we often copy the behaviour we see around us. Our families and traditional culture may present us with one type of behaviour, but advertising can present us with another. Advertisements often portray a particular kind of lifestyle, suggesting ideas that a happy and successful life is one largely based on materialism and consumerism.

Activity

Work in a group to research and analyse some current advertisements.

▲ Many children in modern societies have money of their own to spend.

4.9 Consumer rights

In these lessons you will learn:

- about the rights that are given to consumers
- about the responsibilities placed on consumers
- about laws concerning consumer protection
- to practise using consumer skills.

Consumer rights

When you buy goods or services the law offers you some protection and gives you certain rights. A consumer has a right to:

- be safe from products that might cause ill-effects or injury

- all the information needed to make a good choice

- protection from misleading or dishonest advertising or labelling

- a choice of goods and services offered at **competitive** prices

- receive refunds or similar **compensation** if goods are faulty.

Product safety

Product safety is an important part of **consumer protection**. Governments aim to ensure that all products available to consumers are safe. They do this by creating rules and regulations and setting certain standards. In some countries there are also consumer protection associations.

Foods must be processed, prepared and presented under clean conditions to limit the risk of food poisoning. Toys can have small parts that younger children may swallow, and should not have other features, such as sharp edges, which could cause injury. Electrical goods must be properly manufactured because of the risk of electric shock.

Consumers also need to be told how to use, safely, any products they have purchased.

▲ Many different types of product can present dangers to consumers if they are not properly made, including foods, toys, electrical goods and cars.

Consumer responsibilities

Consumers are also given certain responsibilities and they are expected to:

- find out as much as possible about a product or service before making a purchase

- examine an item carefully before making a purchase

- look for a guarantee

- follow any instructions about how to use a product safely
- purchase goods and services only from genuine and legal sources.

A fair price

In a market there are often a number of goods and services available that are the same or very similar. The people producing these goods or providing these services are said to be in competition with one another to win customers. This competition means that producers, manufacturers and service providers try to get customers to choose their particular brand of goods or the particular service they offer.

Competition is said to be good for the consumer because it means that they will be offered goods and services at competitive prices. These should be honest prices that represent good value.

To keep the competition fair there are often laws to prevent one company becoming a **monopoly** and other laws to prevent companies working together to fix prices.

▲ Manufacturers of similar items compete with one another for a share of the market.

Activities

1 Find out about the work of the government department responsible for consumer protection or about a consumer association in your country.

2 Your family is thinking of buying a new television. Choose a suitable television set and make a case explaining why this is the best one to buy and from where it should be bought.

4.10 The world of work

In this lesson you will learn:
- why people work
- to identify the kinds of work people do in your local area and in the region.

Why do people work?

People work for two main reasons. Firstly, they want to provide for themselves and for their families. Secondly they want to use their skills and talents in a constructive way for something they feel is worthwhile.

Employment in the Arabian Gulf

Traditional employment in the Arabian Gulf countries includes agriculture, crafts, trade and pearl diving.

Oil was discovered in the region in the 1930s and by the 1960s this had become the major source of revenue for many countries in the region. The oil and gas industries are still very important and provide lots of opportunities for different types of work. The income from oil and gas has helped the countries to develop and to create work in other areas.

The development of the countries has required large construction and civil engineering projects which employ many people. As people moved to the region then more industries expanded including financial services, technology, healthcare, retail, education, telecommunications, agriculture and science.

The region is now becoming a tourist destination so there is increasing work in the hospitality and tourism industries.

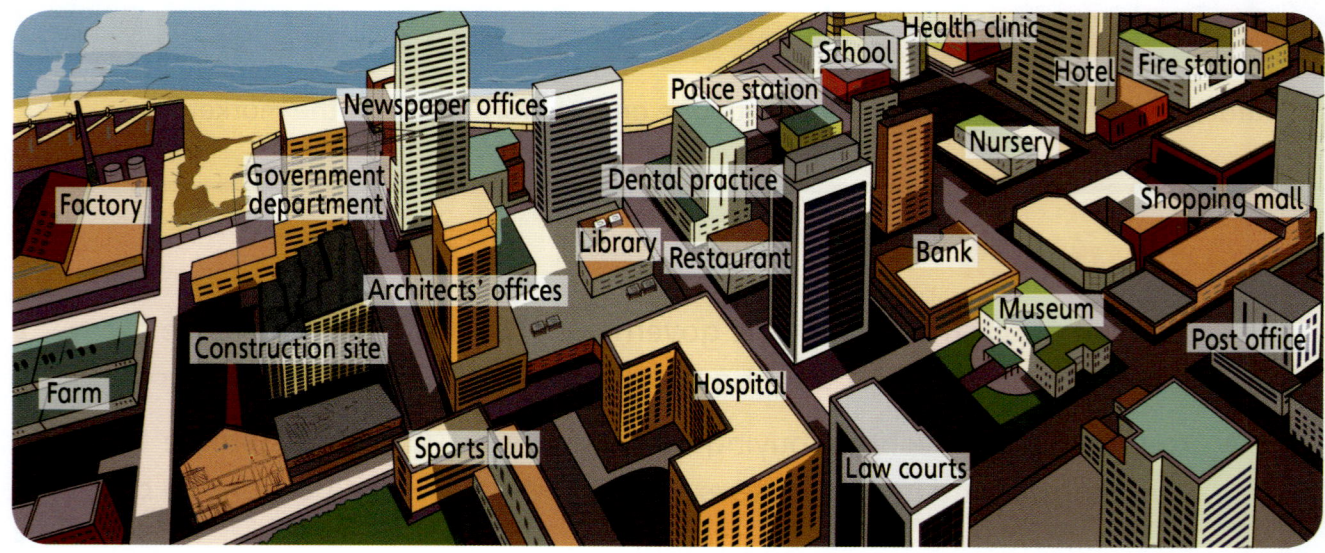

▲ There are many different places to work in and around a modern city.

Different sectors of the economy

PRIMARY SECTOR	
Mining and quarrying	miner, engineer, geologist, safety officer, driver
Agriculture	farm labourer, irrigation engineer, animal expert, machinery operator, plant specialist
Fishing industry	fisherman, marine life expert, fisheries manager, fish farmer
SECONDARY SECTOR	
Processing	oil refinery worker, engineer, chemist, food technology expert, factory manager
Manufacturing	furniture maker, factory manager, electronic equipment maker, safety officer
Construction	architect, builder, plasterer, painter, electrician, plumber
TERTIARY SECTOR	
Commercial services	banking, designing, advertising, transportation, tourist guide, hotel receptionist, waiter
Social services	teacher, kindergarten teacher, school receptionist, social worker, youth worker, doctor, nurse

Who can do what?

Some types of work have traditionally been seen as being more suitable for either men or women. Today men and women work in many different sectors as ideas change. New types of work also arise as a result of computers, technology and **automation**.

Activities

1 Work in a group to discuss the types of job that will be available in the different places shown in the picture on page 92.

2 Write about the criteria that will help you choose the type of work you hope to have in the future. Think about how concerned you are that the job will:

○ be useful and enjoyable

○ suit your skills, temperament and interests

○ be well paid.

4.11 Government systems

In this lesson you will learn:
- about the concept of government
- to describe the functions of government
- to identify different systems of government.

The purpose of government

A country's population is made up of individuals and groups who all have different needs, goals and interests. There needs to be a system to manage and balance all of these. In modern societies this system is the government.

The main purpose of the government is to protect the rights of citizens and to promote the common good. This means that the government should make decisions that are best for the country as a whole and benefit as many people as possible.

▲ Government must understand the needs and desires of its citizens if it is to make good decisions on their behalf.

The functions of government

Providing social services, education, healthcare, welfare and maintaining infrastructure and utilities

Maintaining defence and national security

Maintaining justice, law and order

GOVERNMENT

Raising revenue, budgeting and managing finances

Foreign affairs

Providing support for agriculture and business through subsidies and financial assistance, and creating conditions for economic prosperity

▲ The functions of government.

Government revenue

Some governments raise revenue from direct and indirect taxes and from the sale of state-owned resources to other countries. Some countries also encourage citizens to buy government bonds which support public spending and guarantee a return after a fixed period. The government decides where all this money should be spent.

Systems of government

Monarchy, democracy and dictatorship are the three main types of government.

- In a monarchy, one individual is the monarch or ruler. Rule is usually inherited and passed on within a family. In an absolute monarchy, the ruler has total power and is not controlled by laws or a constitution. Other monarchies operate within a constitution and decisions are made by members of the government. A monarch can be a **head of state** and also the head of government.

- Democracy means 'rule of the people'. In a democracy the people decide how they are going to be governed. The most common form is a representative democracy, where people **vote** in an **election** for certain individuals to represent them. The people who win most votes are given most power to govern and to make laws. These people are made ministers within the government and are given different responsibilities. Democracies often have a number of different political parties.

A political party is a group of people who have similar ideas about what is best for a country and how it should be run. When people vote, they are voting for the political party and not just for an individual.

In a republic, the people elect their representatives and there is an elected or **nominated** president instead of a monarch.

- In a dictatorship one person or group has the power to do whatever they choose and they often take and keep control by use of force. People living under a dictatorship usually have very little freedom.

▲ In a national election, each person casts a vote.

Activity

Find out about and describe the government system in your country and in one other country.

4.12 Government structures

In this lesson you will learn:
- to identify different government structures.

The head of state

The head of state of a country is the highest public representative of the country. In some cases the head of state has a mainly **ceremonial** role but not much power. They represent the country but do not make or control policies.

▲ Heads of state meet to discuss issues at a high level, as at this Afro-Arab summit held in Kuwait in 2013.

The head of government

The head of government is the person who has the highest position of authority in a government and runs the country. In some cases the head of state is also the head of the government.

In a presidential republic, the president is head of state and head of government. In a parliamentary republic, the president is head of state but another person is the head of government.

In a constitutional monarchy, the monarch is head of state but the Prime Minister or Premier is head of government.

Government ministers

A minister is a person who holds an important position within a government. He or she, working with other ministers, can make government policies and put these into practice. Ministers are usually given responsibility for a specific ministry such as education, energy or justice.

Cabinet

The ministers in the different ministries can form a Council of Ministers which is sometimes called the cabinet. A cabinet is often a body that makes policies and decisions. The power of the cabinet varies in different countries.

Countries and states join together

Some countries join together to create a single state, such as the United Kingdom. Some states join together in a **federation** to create a single country, such as India. The federal or central government makes policies and decisions on behalf of all the states. Each state also has some authority to manage its own internal affairs.

Different branches of government

- The Legislative Branch of a government has the power to make laws. This is sometimes known as a parliament or a national assembly.

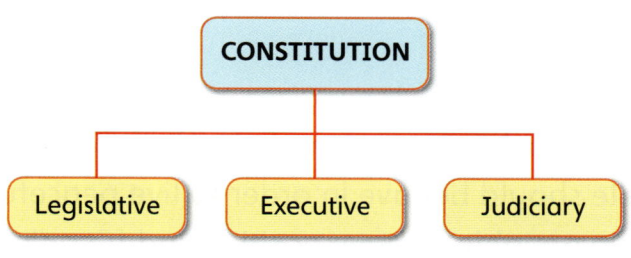

▲ Many countries divide a government up into three sections or 'branches'.

- The Executive Branch has the power to enforce the laws. The head of the government is the head of this branch of government.

- The Judiciary is the branch that decides on the fairness of laws and settles any disagreements about the laws. This branch makes sure that all laws agree with the constitution and that the law is applied fairly to everyone.

One reason for having these separate bodies within a government is to stop any one part of it becoming too powerful. This idea is known as a separation of powers.

Activity

Research the structure of government in your country and in one other country.

In this lesson you will learn:
- to say what laws are
- to explain why laws are needed
- about who makes the laws and how they are made
- about the need for sanctions.

A constitution

A constitution is a document that explains all the ideas and principles that guide law-making. It is used as a reference point and any activity or law that is 'against the constitution' will not be allowed. The constitution also lays out how the country is to be governed, and the powers and authority given to different people or groups. In many Islamic nations, the constitution and other laws are based on Sharia.

Laws

Rules made by a government are known as laws. Laws make it clear how people should behave in order to live peacefully and safely together. If people are able to have positive and friendly relations it produces a society in which there is harmony and order.

▲ Laws help people to live without fear.

Laws should apply to everyone in the same way. There are not different or special laws for certain groups of people. In this way the laws provide guidance and protection for everyone equally. Governments are responsible for making sure this happens.

Laws are used to control the way in which people behave and to protect the rights of individuals. Governments actually make laws but the ideas for laws can come from different sources, including an individual. New laws are introduced when a different set of circumstances emerges and has to be dealt with. Laws can also be changed or removed completely for similar reasons or if they are considered to be unfair.

Laws are about helping to keep people safe and healthy and to prevent them from being treated badly or dishonestly. Laws allow people to live without fear and to have a fair chance to make the most of their potential. Without laws, people who are stronger or more powerful would simply be able to do what they wanted.

Laws work partly because there is a system of punishments for those who break them. If a person is accused of breaking a law they are entitled to have a fair hearing or trial. If it is proved that they have broken the law then there will be consequences for this, such as the payment of a fine or a prison sentence.

Helping to maintain law and order

There are systems within each country which enforce the laws that governments have introduced, and maintain the order that the laws are supposed to create. The organisation that does most to prevent crime and maintain law and order is the police. There is also a system of courts and judges in which people accused of crime can be put on trial.

◄ The police are an important part of the system of law and order.

> ## Activity
>
> Work as a class to produce a set of principles and values that will help you create a classroom constitution.

4.14 Education

In this lesson you will learn:
- about the range of human resources available
- how education is used to develop human resources

Human resources

The people in the population of a country are sometimes called its human resources or its human capital. People are resources because they can use their skills, time, abilities and energies in different ways to benefit the country.

▲ Governments want to make the best use of human resources just as they do any other resources.

People can contribute to a society by:

- working in any of the many occupations available
- making it possible for others to go out to work, for example by providing childcare
- creating works of art
- by developing human resources, for example by working in education or healthcare.

Education

Education allows each individual to develop their own particular skills and talents. By doing this they are able to make the most of their potential for themselves as individuals and as members of a society. Education improves people's chances of having a productive life and of being able to provide for themselves and their families.

Education informs people of the values and ideas that are important in society and helps them to understand the roles and responsibilities they have. They also learn to develop the knowledge, thinking and decision-making skills and attributes that will help them to fulfil these roles.

Education takes place at different levels or stages, as children grow and develop.

Pre-school education

Research shows that pre-school education is a very important stage of learning. Children gain some basic knowledge and skills in language, mathematics and find out about the world. They also learn physical, creative and interpersonal skills.

Primary and secondary education

As students rise through primary and secondary education they should be building a range of skills, knowledge, attitudes and abilities that will assist them as they either move on to further study or into the workplace. At the higher levels, students begin to focus their studies on a smaller range of subjects of their choosing.

▲ As we grow older we begin to think about what work we might do in the future.

Tertiary education

Tertiary education takes place in training colleges and universities. Students specialise in studying a particular subject area that will help them enter a particular occupation or give them a set of useful skills and knowledge that could be useful in a range of jobs.

▲ Tertiary education is available in many subjects throughout the Arabian Gulf region.

Activity

Write a brief explanation of why individuals have a responsibility to themselves and to society to make the most of their education.

4.15 Human resources – health

The importance of health

A person who is fit and healthy is able to enjoy life more fully and will experience less personal suffering, and this is obviously a good thing. The health of the individuals in a population is also important to society as a whole. This is because a person's health affects his or her ability to work and determines the amount of resources used in providing healthcare.

For these reasons, as well as personal happiness, a person has a responsibility to do everything possible to remain healthy.

Promoting good health

Governments spend money on promoting good health practices among the population.

Some governments face the challenge of ensuring that there is enough food to feed the population. In other countries the governments face the challenge of helping people to make healthy choices about the food they eat, and to avoid eating too much.

Diets in the past were often very simple and based on what people were able to provide for themselves as families or as groups within a community. Today most people do not provide their own food and much of what is bought includes many items that are not particularly healthy because they are high in fats, sugar or salt.

▲ Many foods today are high in fats, sugar or salt.

Governments today are also becoming aware of the need to address people's mental health and wellbeing.

Governments also have to address the fact that people today are very inactive. In the past people were much more likely to walk to the places they needed to go to, and most activities involved physical effort. Labour-saving devices, such as washing machines, have removed the need for physical activity in simple household chores.

Preventive healthcare

Preventive healthcare is about preventing disease, illness and injury. Promoting a healthy lifestyle is part of this, alongside other parts of health education. Other approaches, such as a vaccination programme, seek to eliminate the dangers of particular diseases. Access to safe drinking water and good sanitation facilities are also important.

Health services

Governments also seek to ensure that proper health services are provided. These provide the care and treatment people need if they have a problem with their health, such as a disease or injury. Health services are provided in hospitals, health centres and clinics.

Activity

Work in a group to find out about the health services in your country.

▲ Health services are often delivered through hospitals, clinics and health centres.

4.16 Public safety

In this lesson you will learn:
- to identify matters of public safety
- about the role of the emergency services.

Public safety

Governments have a responsibility to put measures in place that will help to protect the safety of the population and to address problems resulting from accidents and natural disasters. They introduce laws to address particular situations such as dangerous driving, building safety and the handling and storage of dangerous materials. They also promote safety awareness through public information campaigns.

There will still be times when accidents occur and when safety is threatened by natural events. For these situations, the government ensures that adequate emergency services are in place. These can be provided directly by the government or by companies operating on its behalf.

Governments often have a ministry responsible for internal security. This usually has a department for dealing with emergencies and protecting public safety.

▲ Why do there need to be rules and regulations about transporting dangerous materials?

Police

The police have a number of roles directly related to maintaining public safety. Countries are safer places if there is 'the rule of law' and where 'law and order' is kept. In such countries people obey the laws and the police offer protection against the dangers of criminal activity.

The police are there to protect personal safety and the safety of property. Their work involves enforcing the law by bringing those who break laws to justice but they also seek to prevent crime and enhance safety through awareness campaigns.

Fire and rescue services

As well as the important job of putting out fires, the fire and rescue services also respond to emergency situations. This can include incidents involving dangerous substances such as flammable fuels or dangerous chemicals. Members of these services will also be called upon to rescue people from dangerous situations following an accident or a natural disaster.

The personnel in these services become experts in what causes fires, the different ways in which fires burn and how best each type of fire can be extinguished. They are therefore able to give advice on fire prevention and safety.

Emergency medical services

Emergency medical services, such as paramedics and the ambulance service, will usually be the responsibility of a Ministry or Council of Health. Paramedics are specially trained to provide care or seek to prolong a person's life following an accident or sudden illness, before they reach a hospital.

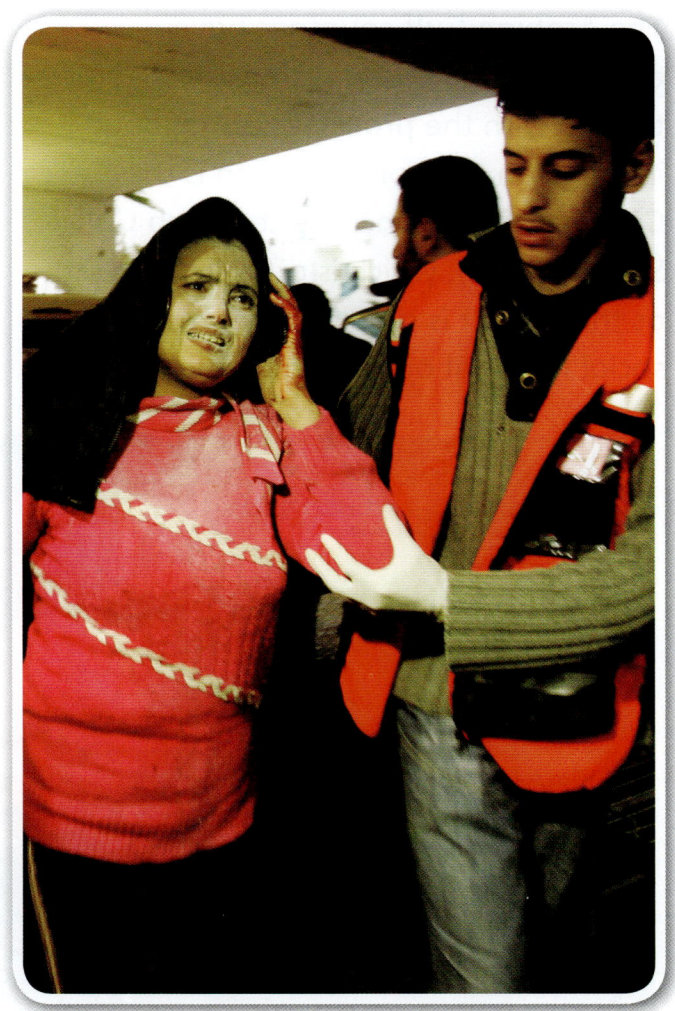

▲ Emergency medical care is provided by paramedics and ambulance services.

Activity

Find out about the work of one of the emergency services in your country.

4.17 The GCC

In this lesson you will learn:
- about the organisation created to enable regional co-operation.

The Co-operation Council for the Arab Gulf States (AGCC)

The Arabian Gulf countries have established an organisation which aims to help with the processes of regional integration. This organisation is the Co-operation Council for the Arab Gulf States (AGCC), which is often referred to as the GCC. It is a political, economic and social regional organisation which aims to assist in processes of regional co-operation. It was established on 4 February 1981 and held its first summit on 25 May 1981.

Members of the GCC are:
- The United Arab Emirates
- The State of Bahrain
- The Kingdom of Saudi Arabia
- The Sultanate of Oman
- The State of Qatar
- The State of Kuwait.

▲ The flag of the GCC.

Objectives of the GCC

The basic objectives of the Co-operation Council are:

- To bring about the co-ordination of member states in order to achieve unity among them.
- To strengthen relations among people in each country.
- To put together similar regulations in a number of fields including:
  - economic and financial affairs
  - commerce, customs and communications
  - education and culture
  - social and health affairs
  - information and tourism
  - legislative and administrative affairs.
- To stimulate scientific and technological progress, to establish scientific research and joint ventures, and to encourage co-operation by the private sector for the good of all people.

The structure of the GCC

The Supreme Council is the highest authority in the GCC. Its purpose is to:

- create policies at the highest level
- review the recommendations and reports received from the Ministerial Council
- approve the rules and guidance for dealing with other states at an international level.

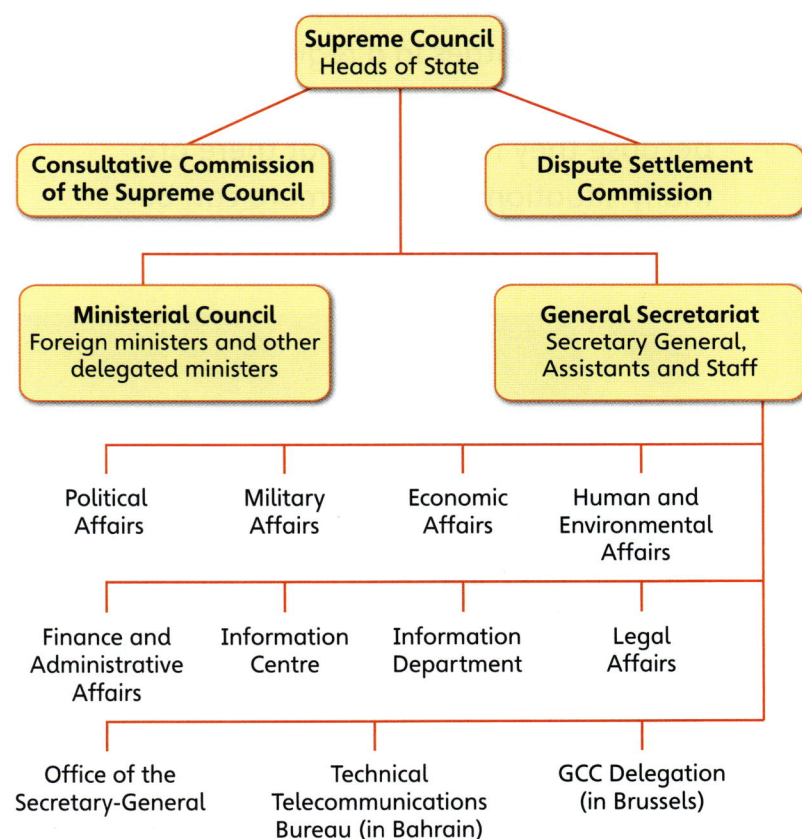

▲ Structure of the GCC.

Activities

1 Write down the current members of the Supreme Council of the GCC.

2 Make a booklet that could be provided to the public to inform them of the GCC and its main functions. Begin by writing briefly about the member countries.

In these lessons you will learn:

- to consider the values and goals that bring the region together
- how countries can work together within the region
- to identify the benefits of countries co-operating with one another.

Regional co-operation

Regional co-operation happens when separate countries in a region work together and co-operate. They do this because they recognise that there are many situations in which more can be achieved by countries working together rather than alone. For example, they can work together on joint projects in different areas of life, or make sure the work they are doing is co-ordinated.

When countries co-operate they sometimes make it easier for people and goods to move across their borders.

▲ The countries of the Arabian Peninsula share many borders and have common traditions and cultures.

Advantages of co-operation in the Arabian Gulf countries

In the countries of the Arabian Gulf there are obvious ties to do with a shared Arab heritage and a common religion. Regional co-operation strengthens these ties and also aims to make the best possible use of the resources available so that the region becomes more self-sufficient.

Economic co-operation

A country's economy is all human economic activity involved in creating, buying and using the goods and services that are created and used within a country. The consumers within a country make up the 'domestic market'. A small population means that there is a small domestic market. As businesses grow they need a larger market and this can be created when countries co-operate. If they agree, then goods from one country can be sold in all the other regional countries. This means that there is now a much larger regional market.

Other measures can be put in place to help producers in the region.

For example, goods that are imported often have a tax or **duty** placed on them. It is possible for countries to agree to remove any import duty on goods arriving from countries with whom they are co-operating.

By working together, countries in a region can be in a stronger position when they negotiate with other countries or regional **blocs**.

The countries of the Arabian Gulf also share the benefits of having access to oil and gas. They co-operate to make sure that all policies about the oil and gas industries – for example to do with exploration, extraction, marketing and pricing – are in harmony.

At the same time, individual countries want to see a wider range of industries and jobs available, and working together means that similar rules will apply in all countries in the region.

Economic co-operation also involves introducing and using similar rules and regulations for other businesses and systems across the region, including transportation, telecommunications, water and agriculture.

◀ It is sensible to co-ordinate the planning and construction of the regional transport network.

Political co-operation

The countries of the Arabian Gulf have their own governments. This does not change when there is regional political co-operation. Co-operation means that the different governments agree to work together on certain projects and to support and encourage one another. Regional co-operation also means that the countries present a unified response to developments and situations in the wider world.

Cultural co-operation

The countries of the region share a great deal in terms of their traditions and cultures, which can be seen in the shared values and characteristics of the populations. Cultural co-operation aims to help citizens of all these countries to treasure their own cultural heritage as an individual nation and also to see that it is part of a shared Arab/Islamic cultural heritage.

Countries in the region work together to put on co-ordinated or joint events and to take part in shared activities. These cover a wide range of cultural expression, including creative arts and Arab calligraphy, literature, music, poetry, theatre and dance.

Culture is also about preserving and celebrating cultural heritage. Countries work together on strategies to do with identifying and preserving ancient sites and objects, and the use of museums. Museums are not simply places where objects can be displayed. They are also places of education where people can learn about the past.

◀ Different places are celebrated as Capitals of Islamic Culture for the region and the wider Arab Muslim world. Nizwa in Oman had this honour in 2015.

Educational co-operation

Co-operation in education helps the countries of the Arabian Gulf to develop and share the best ideas available in education.

Founded in 1975, the Arab Bureau of Education for the Gulf States (ABEGS), located in Riyadh, is an intergovernmental regional organisation that works within the six member states (Saudi Arabia, the United Arab Emirates, Bahrain, Kuwait, Oman and Qatar). The organisation seeks to promote co-operation and co-ordination in the fields of culture, education, science, information and documentation.

In practical terms this co-operation also means that students from one country can receive an education in another. This means that if a student wishes to undertake a degree in a subject that is not taught at a university in their own country, they can travel to another country where it is taught.

▲ Regional co-operation in education can help ensure that all students have access to education.

Medical co-operation

Medical co-operation is about making sure that the best possible healthcare is available across the region. All the region's countries are facing similar challenges, such as growing populations, ageing populations and increases in certain types of illness. Because the populations have grown so quickly there is also a challenge to have enough skilled and trained staff available. The governments of the Arabian Gulf countries are constantly improving and increasing the opportunities for medical training and education. The hope is that this will enable more people from the region to become qualified health professionals who want to stay and work in the region.

Medical co-operation means that:

- the available resources will be well used

- health services are planned and provided in similar ways across the region

- the health services save money

- medicines and medical equipment can be bought in greater quantities, and therefore at a better price.

Another good reason for neighbouring countries to work together is that illnesses and diseases, and the insects and other animals that sometimes carry them, do not confine themselves within the borders of a country. Medical co-operation is essential in combating diseases and controlling their spread. Countries can help one another by putting in place suitable processes for detection, monitoring, prevention and treatment.

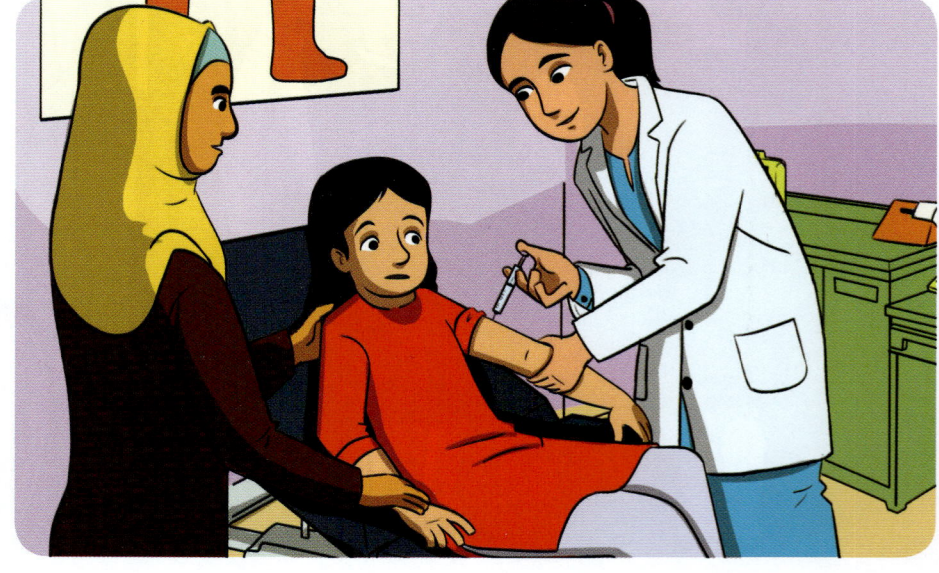

▲ It is sensible for neighbouring countries to work together to take preventive measures such as immunising people against a particular disease.

Scientific and technical co-operation

GCC members see that science and technology are essential for development and welfare and so progress in these areas is a priority. There are many programmes to develop the potential for the region in science, technology and research.

Once again the aim of co-operation is to co-ordinate the work being done so that there is no unnecessary duplication and to make sure that all resources are used efficiently and effectively. Governments can:

- provide funds for research directly
- encourage research within the private sector
- establish systems that make sure information is shared freely between countries.

Co-operation for security

Countries of the Arabian Gulf feel that they face similar challenges to their security. As a result they have agreed to co-operate in creating armed forces that will deter and respond to any military threats or other threats to the security of any member state of the GCC.

These forces have the same training and education and follow the same operating procedures. They carry out military exercises together and countries aim to have military systems and items of equipment that can be used by all of the states.

Activity

Add information which describes some of the objectives of co-operation to your booklet about the GCC (see page 107).

Unit 4 Review questions

1. Which statement defines a monarchy?
   a. The ruler is elected by the people.
   b. The ruler inherits power from his family.
   c. The ruler is a military leader who takes power.
   d. The ruler is elected by a national parliament.

2. A group that tries to influence government and public opinion is:
   a. a community group
   b. an interest group
   c. a pressure group
   d. a charity

3. Copy out the true statement.
   a. People buying local goods leads to more exports.
   b. People buying foreign goods will help local businesses.
   c. People buying local food brings about food security.
   d. People buying local goods will reduce imports.

4. It is a human right that everyone should be able to:
   a. watch a film once a week
   b. drink clean water
   c. go to university
   d. drive a car

5. Which of these habitats in the Arabian Gulf need special protection?
   a. Mangrove swamps
   b. Rainforests
   c. Public parks
   d. Date palm plantations

6. In some government systems the part that interprets the law and holds criminal trials is the:
   a. legislature
   b. executive
   c. judiciary

7. Draw a diagram showing the three main parts of the structure of the GCC.

8. Name the three sectors of the economy. Give an example of one type of work for each sector.

9. Briefly describe two ways in which a government develops a country's human resources.

10. Explain two benefits of regional co-operation in the GCC countries.

11. Describe two ways in which you think you can be a good citizen.

12. Write about an environmental problem you are aware of in your country and suggest two ideas that would help to address that problem.

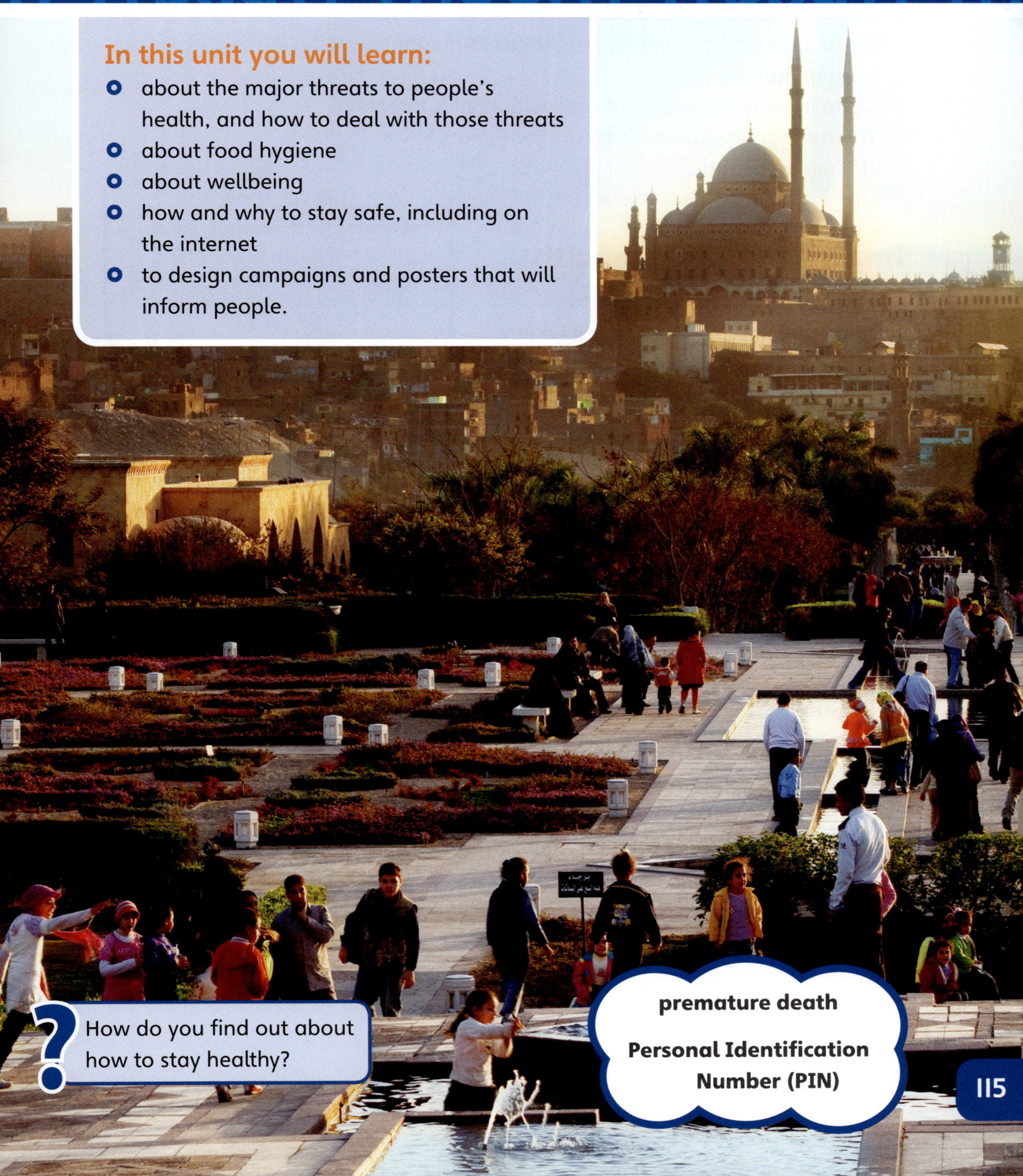

5 Health and wellbeing

In this unit you will learn:
- about the major threats to people's health, and how to deal with those threats
- about food hygiene
- about wellbeing
- how and why to stay safe, including on the internet
- to design campaigns and posters that will inform people.

? How do you find out about how to stay healthy?

premature death

Personal Identification Number (PIN)

5.1 Major health problems

In this lesson you will learn:
- to identify the major health threats to human populations
- to identify the causes of the major health threats
- to suggest solutions to the major threats to
- human health.

Improvements in health

As a country develops, it is able to promote and improve the general health of its population. Improvements happen for a number of reasons. For example, the population has access to enough food to avoid undernourishment, and to a variety of food that ensures people get all the different nutrients they need. The population will also have access to clean water for drinking and good sanitation systems. These allow people to wash away germs and get rid of waste, which helps prevent the spread of diseases.

As they develop, countries are also better able to inform and educate their populations about health issues. They can also provide better health services to prevent and treat illnesses. In these societies there are fewer deaths of babies and young children, less illness and people tend to live longer.

Communicable and contagious diseases

Communicable and contagious diseases are those that can be passed from one person to another. This can happen when people are in direct contact or when there is an exchange of bodily fluids, for example through a sneeze or cough. Diseases can also sometimes be spread by insects such as mosquitoes.

▲ Sneezing or coughing into a tissue catches the germs.

These diseases are dealt with in three main ways:

- prevention of the diseases, for example through immunisation or through the use of such items as mosquito nets or the provision of clean water

- treatment of the disease when and where medicines exist

- education programmes to inform people about symptoms of the diseases, how they are spread and how they can be treated.

▲ Washing hands regularly is an important part of preventing the spread of disease.

Non-communicable diseases (NCDs)

Non-communicable diseases (NCDs) are not infectious and cannot be transmitted between people. They include heart disease, many cancers, asthma, diabetes and high blood pressure. The World Health Organisation (WHO) figures suggest that NCDs are the world's biggest killers. They account for 63% of all deaths worldwide and cause many **premature deaths**.

▲ Choosing a healthy lifestyle reduces the risk of suffering from one of the non-communicable diseases.

NCDs are associated with a number of risk factors which are mostly to do with the way people live. The main risks are tobacco use, an unhealthy diet (high in sugar, fats and salt), lack of physical exercise and the harmful use of alcohol.

Unfortunately this is a global problem and the countries of the Arabian Gulf are no exception. There has been a dramatic increase in the occurrence of these diseases and they are now the leading cause of death in the GCC countries.

Activity

Design a poster that informs people of one of the common threats to health and how these can be avoided.

5.2 Food hygiene and health

In this lesson you will learn:
- to identify the major health risks from food
- about food hygiene
- how people are informed about food hygiene.

Food and health

A healthy diet contains a mixture of foods and a high proportion of fruit and vegetables. The benefits of eating such a diet are well known and the dangers of eating a diet that is high in fats, sugar and salt are also clear. Other health problems are associated with food when it is contaminated.

▲ Food items like fruit go rotten after a while. This process involves many tiny bacteria which it would not be good to have in your body.

Bacteria can be found everywhere – in the air, in water, in soil and on our bodies. Some bacteria are helpful and help parts of our bodies, such as our digestive system, to work properly. However, some bacteria are unhelpful because they cause diseases. Some foods can contain harmful bacteria which may be in the food to begin with or may be picked up by the food while it is being stored, transported or prepared. Many fresh foods need to be kept cool to stop harmful bacteria from breeding on them. When the food contains harmful germs, either bacteria or viruses, these are taken into the body when the food is eaten.

If this happens people can suffer from food poisoning. Food poisoning is unpleasant because it can cause an upset stomach and reactions such as vomiting or diarrhoea. In extreme cases it can result in death.

▲ Most bacteria on foods can be removed by careful washing or cooking.

Avoiding food poisoning

There are a number of simple steps to reduce the risks of food poisoning:

- Eat and use food when it is fresh. Packaged food may have a label giving a date by when the food should be used.

- Never eat food that looks, smells or tastes as though it might be off.

- Store food according to the advice on labels, and always keep raw foods away from cooked foods or ready-to-eat foods such as cheese or salad.

- Wash fresh fruit and vegetables to remove any soil or residues of chemicals or germs from other people who may have handled the food.

- When preparing food, avoid 'cross-contamination' by using separate utensils and chopping boards for different food types. Always wash these thoroughly after use.

- Wash hands before, during and after food preparation, especially after handling raw meat, fish and poultry.

- Make sure foods are cooked according to any instructions. The high temperatures involved in cooking will kill any germs in food that could be harmful.

▲ Different types of foods should be prepared using separate boards and equipment.

Activity

Design a poster to go in a restaurant or school kitchen to inform people of the food hygiene rules.

5.3 What is wellbeing?

In this lesson you will learn:
- to identify the things that contribute to wellbeing
- why wellbeing is important to individuals
- why governments are concerned with the wellbeing of a population.

What is wellbeing?

People have wondered about wellbeing for thousands of years. The idea really concerns what each person thinks about the quality of his or her life and how much satisfaction it brings. It is an attempt to address some of the ideas around what it means to be a human being and what each person should do with his or her life.

It is felt that for people to have a sense of wellbeing they need to:

- have a sense of enjoying life simply because they are alive

- be involved with activities which they find engaging and meaningful

- have a sense of personal control and feelings of self-confidence and of their own abilities

- possess some inner strength and other attributes that will help them to cope in difficult circumstances and to deal with changes that occur outside their control.

▲ There are times when it feels good just being alive.

It is also assumed that wellbeing improves when a person engages with other people and with his or her surroundings. At the same time, that sense of wellbeing helps a person to enjoy those interactions. It also helps people to think creatively and to rise to challenges. In this sense it is a resource. It is also an ultimate goal for which people strive.

Wellbeing and society

Societies are often assessed using different sets of criteria, for example the general health of the population. Another common measure is the amount of economic activity. This is the simple idea that if a country's economy is growing then the population will be enjoying a better life. If people have money and have material possessions then there is a good chance that they will feel better than if they have little or no money and cannot afford the things they need.

However, there is evidence to suggest that people's level of happiness or sense of wellbeing only improves until a certain level of material comfort is reached. After that point, the accumulation of wealth and possessions does little or nothing to improve wellbeing because other factors, such as relationships and feeling safe, influence the individual much more strongly.

▲ Meaningful relationships are one of the most important factors that affect our sense of wellbeing.

One purpose of government is to enhance the wellbeing of the population. To do this they try to understand the factors that affect wellbeing and create appropriate policies.

Activities

1 Write about your sense of wellbeing using the factors listed above.

2 Work in a group to suggest some policies that a government could introduce to improve people's sense of wellbeing.

In this lesson you will learn:

- to identify real-life situations where we need to be aware of safety
- to identify ways in which we can stay safe in these situations.

Personal responsibility

It's a fact: life is full of risk. There are potential hazards and dangers everywhere and in almost any situation.

Some of these situations are outside the control of any individual person. We often have to rely on other people to make sure that what they are doing does not put other people in danger.

Some situations are outside of anyone's control, for example natural disasters. In the case of natural disaster, governments and other bodies may have taken measures to prepare for the situation. Warnings may have been issued and there may be some facilities available which might offer protection or shelter.

In all situations an individual must take some responsibility for his or her own safety. Each person should know the measures that can be taken to make sure he or she is as safe as possible in any particular situation. Much of this is down to decisions about behaviour and attitudes towards other people.

▲ We have to rely on other people to obey traffic laws, to drive safely and to have well-maintained vehicles.

▲ People can be made aware of dangers but each person must still choose to behave in a way that does not put him or herself in danger.

Dangers in the environment

People suffer injuries when they are hit, when they hit a hard surface or if they are cut. This is a result of the structure of our bodies which include bones that can break, joints that can come apart and soft tissue that is easily damaged.

This means that simple things such as hard surfaces and sharp edges can damage our body. It means there is the potential for injury almost everywhere. An important part of growing up is finding out about these everyday hazards and learning ways of minimising the risk of injury.

The potential for more serious injury increases as we travel faster, are higher off the ground or are on or in the water. We need to take extra care in these situations. In the same way, if we are handling things that we know pose a danger, such as glass, sharp knives or chemicals, we again have to pay special attention to what we are doing.

If we are with other people then there is someone to help us if things go wrong.

Dangers from other people

It is a sad fact that we can sometimes face danger from other people who deliberately want to harm us or hurt us. It is always a good idea to be with relatives or a friend when out in public places and to tell your family where you plan to go and who you will be with.

▲ A person is less vulnerable in a group. If something does happen to one person, others are able to summon help.

Activities

1. Work in a group to identify the hazards that exist in your school, your home, in the street, in public spaces and near water.

2. Choose one area and write some guidance for people on ways in which they can be safe.

3. Find out about a safety campaign in your area.

In this lesson you will learn:
- to identify potential dangers on the internet
- to identify ways in which we can stay safe in these situations.

Safety on the internet is about protecting your computer, protecting your personal information and protecting yourself.

Protecting your computer

Computers work using software. This is a set of instructions that can be read by the computer which tell it what actions to perform. System software is used to actually run the operations of the computer. Application software is used to perform work, such as word processing, or to allow the user to access entertainment, such as music or games.

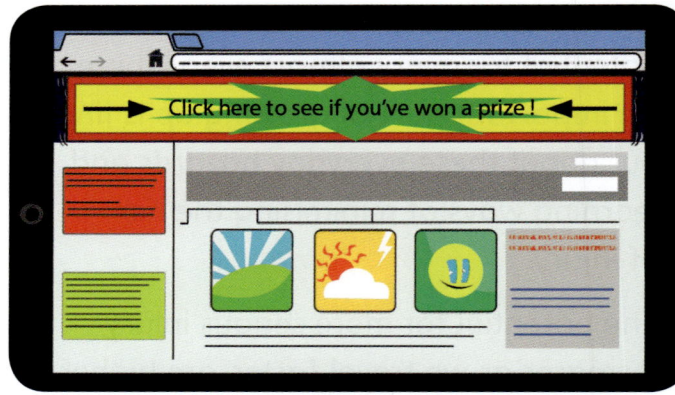

▲ It is sensible not to click on links that don't look as though they can be trusted.

Malicious software or 'malware' is designed to cause damage or disruption to a computer. Malware is often used by people using computers for criminal activity such as fraud. A malware program is known as a virus when it is able to make copies of itself and then send these to other computers which 'infects' them with the same malware.

Malware can be added to email attachments and can be linked to advertisements or special offers that appear on web pages.

Protecting your personal information

An individual's personal information includes things like his or her real name, address, email address, phone number and computer passwords. People also have financial information such as bank account details and **PIN numbers** for debit or credit cards. People who are a threat to others on the internet want to obtain this information for bad reasons.

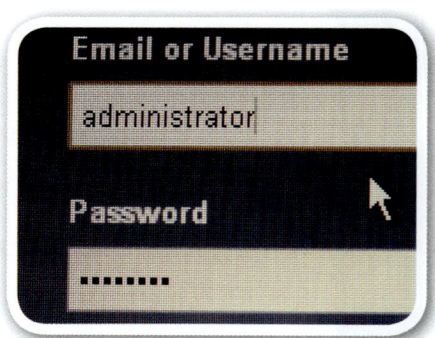

▲ Personal information should only be entered on trusted sites.

Personal safety

Using the internet can pose a threat to our physical wellbeing and to our emotional wellbeing. Our physical wellbeing can be directly threatened if we spend too much time using the internet and do not allow enough time for physical activity.

◀ Using the computer for a long time means people are not being physically active.

We can also put ourselves in danger if we agree to meet anyone we have only known online. It is never a good idea to do this because we do not know who people really are from the identity they have provided online.

Our emotional wellbeing can be damaged if we see material that causes us to be upset or offended. Sadly, some individuals also use the internet to deliberately say unkind and hurtful things about other people.

Activities

1 Carry out interviews to find out how aware people are of internet safety.

2 Work in a group to devise an internet safety campaign.

Unit 5 Review questions

1 A disease that is contagious is:
a passed on from one person to another
b caused by eating bad food
c caused by drinking dirty water
d only a problem in childhood

2 Which is the true statement about bacteria?
a All bacteria are bad for you.
b There are no bacteria in frozen raw chicken.
c Bacteria breed fastest in warm conditions.
d Bacteria cannot survive in water.

3 Copy out the true statement.
a Eating a high-fat diet can reduce the risk of developing a non-communicable disease.
b Non-communicable diseases are only a problem for people who do not eat properly.
c Regular exercise is a good way to reduce the risk of developing a non-communicable disease.
d Non-communicable diseases are only a problem for elderly people.

4 You should dry your hands after washing them because:
a wet hands will get cold
b wet hands will drip water on the floor
c wet hands can't hold things properly
d germs spread more easily on wet hands

5 Wellbeing is about:
a having a lot of money
b feeling that your life has purpose
c being fit and healthy
d being an important person

6 Answer 'Yes' or 'No' to the following questions:
a I have met a person online and they say they would like to meet. Should I go?
b A website wants my email address and phone number so that I can enter a competition. Should I enter these details?
c A friend of mine wants me to send a digital photo of myself. Should I?
d I get an email from a company that says I could win a prize if I enter the code word contained in an attachment. Should I open the attachment?

7 Describe three real-life situations where people need to be aware of safety and explain how they can stay safe.

8 Write about two ways in which you are responsible for your own safety around the school.

Glossary

astronomy the scientific study of the position and movement of stars, moons and planets

automation the use of machines to do work that was previously done by people

axis an imaginary line through the centre of an object, around which the object turns

bank an organisation that provides various financial services, for example keeping or lending money

bloc a group of countries that work together because they have similar interests

breeding in plants, the science of growing plants to have desired characteristics

ceremonial when a person has little or no power in his or her role but mainly attends religious and public occasions

charity giving help to those in need, often in the form of money

climate the typical atmospheric conditions over an extended period of time

compensation the act of giving money to someone for a loss of some kind

competitive as good as or even better than similar examples

consumer protection a system including laws and regulations designed to protect consumer rights

cosmetics beauty products, such as lipstick, sometimes called 'make-up'

cyclone a violent storm in which strong winds move in a circle

desertification process in which land slowly becomes desert

dialect the form of a language that is spoken by people living in a particular region or social group

duty a tax on the goods that are imported to a country

dynasty a series of rulers from the same family

election an organised event where people vote for a certain person to represent them

elevation height above the ground

federation a group of states sharing a centralised government but with freedom over certain internal affairs

fertility in plants, the level of ability to produce new fruit or plants

festival a day or period of the year when people stop working to celebrate a special event, often a religious one

head of state the official leader of a country who is sometimes also the leader of the government

irrigation a means of supplying water to growing crops through a system of pipes, channels or tunnels

latitude describing the angle of a location above or below the line of the equator (0° latitude)

lobby to attempt to influence a person or an organisation on an issue

longitude describing the angle of a location either east or west of the Prime Meridian (0° longitude)

magnetic field an area around a magnet or magnetic object, where there is a force that will attract some metals towards it

modernisation to make methods or ideas more suitable for use at the present time

monopoly the complete control of trade in particular goods or the supply of a particular service

navigation the process of accurately determining one's position and of planning routes

nominated chosen for a particular position or prize

passport an official document issued by a government that identifies a person as a citizen of a particular country

Personal Identification Number (PIN) a number usually given by a bank and used for payments or when taking money from a cash machine

pesticide a substance, usually a chemical, used for destroying insects or plants that are harmful to crops

pollution substances in the environment that have harmful or poisonous characteristics

premature death dying at an age before that which could be reasonably expected of a healthy person

ratio the relationship between a measurement between two locations identified on a map, and the actual distance on the ground between those two locations

revenue the money that a government receives from taxes or that an organisation receives from its business

siege a military operation in which an army tries to capture a town by surrounding it and cutting off supplies to the people inside

social media websites and application software that allow users to create and share content across a social network

spouse a husband or wife

suburbs a residential area where people live that is outside the centre of a city

tax money paid to the government as a contribution to state revenue

thrift saving money and spending it carefully so that it is not wasted

toll money paid for using a particular bridge or road

urbanisation the process in which greater proportions of a population move to live in cities rather than in rural areas

vizier an important official in certain Muslim government systems

vote a choice that people make to indicate a preference for one person, proposal or situation over another